honey

"Bee-Inspired"
Cheers

honey

BeesOnline Recipe Collection

maureen maxwell

photography scott venning

TANDEM PRESS

First published in New Zealand in 2003 by
Tandem Press
PO Box 34 272
Birkenhead, Auckland
New Zealand
www.tandempress.co.nz

National Library of New Zealand Cataloguing-in-Publication Data

Maxwell, Maureen.
Honey : BeesOnline recipe collection / Maureen Maxwell.
Includes index.
ISBN 1-877298-14-X
1. Cookery (Honey) I. BeesOnline. II. Title.
641.68 — dc 21

Design by Nick Turzynski
Printed in New Zealand by Brebner Print Limited

This book is dedicated to my family, to my mother who taught me about wonderful fresh food and has always encouraged all my cooking endeavours, and for my children Rachael and Ryan, who one day just might need my recipes.

contents

introduction

Honey is almost magically created by bees from the nectar of flowers and has occupied a central place in culinary, cultural and medicinal history. Long before cave dwellers sketched images of honey hunters on walls, bees and their extraordinary tiered social structure were working to transform the very essence of our landscape, encapsulating in wax pure energy, aroma and taste.

From having one beehive in my backyard I have launched into an amazing adventure. In just four short years, I have established the BeesOnline brand and export market. Based at Waimauku, on the West Coast, just 30 minutes from Auckland's CBD, we run a fully sustainable organic factory site. From here we proudly service a global market and welcome visitors to our very successful retail shop and café.

A country girl at heart, I found that a beehive was the answer for my ailing fruit trees. The first taste of my own fresh honey harvested on a warm autumn day was like a taste explosion. The nuances of flavour were so exciting. My wine-tasting skills to the fore, I learnt to appreciate the varietals and regional differences as I searched for other honey types. Honey is so complex in flavour, texture and aroma. Weather influences and the foraging range of the colony produce individual characteristics as exciting as premium estate-bottled wine. Honey, like wine, takes time to appreciate, with the complexities transforming as it matures.

Humans cannot replicate honey. It is a 'super-food' that can be used directly from the hive. It is pure, slow food at its best — no additives or preservatives required. The nectar is ingested, mixed with enzymes and a little body heat, then placed in the most amazing wax packaging for ripening, sealed only when it attains the correct moisture content.

Honey, like pollen, is gathered by bees to feed the workers and brood. Each generation contributes to the survival of the colony. The beehive is an extraordinary example of social order, the population being controlled by the environment. When conditions are fine and the nectar is flowing, the queen lays with great haste to increase the hive numbers, thus making optimum use of the available harvest. As the honey flow comes to an end and the weather cools, laying slows so that only a core crew protects the queen and hive over the long winter months, surviving on the stored resources or extra food that may be provided by the beekeeper in times of adverse conditions. As a new spring unfolds, the cycle starts all over again, as the hive bursts into action, tripling in size to provide the necessary workforce to pollinate and collect nectar for the coming season.

The hive has been a quintessential element of our ecosystem throughout history, pollinating a vast variety of plants. In New Zealand the honey bee (*Apis mellifera*) is attributed with 90 percent of all insect pollination, so is a vital party to our agricultural and horticultural industries, contributing billions of dollars to the economy annually. It has become vital for the contemporary beekeeper to support bee colonies as the loss of natural habitat, pesticides and the deadly varroa mite epidemic decimate our bee populations.

At BeesOnline we strive to assist the hives in this time of environmental change, protecting and nurturing the colonies through harsh winters and food shortages, moving hives to nectar and pollen sources. Our team harvest organically and seek to present this valuable natural resource in ways to tempt the palate. Each harvest is unique, reflecting the nectar source and season. A chunk of new-season honeycomb embodies the essence and warmth of a sweet summer's day, turning the beauty of the flower into luscious pools of flavour.

The virtues of honey are immense and have been well documented throughout history with new research regularly uncovering additional benefits, and I have found it an exciting challenge to update traditional lore and educate people about the benefits of including honey in our daily diet.

My cooking is strongly influenced by season, region, and the integrity of ingredients as well as respect for the environment. For this reason I choose to use fresh organic produce (including free-range eggs) whenever possible.

I am often called upon to address chefs both in New Zealand and overseas, and in response to many requests I have composed this honey collection to illustrate the versatility of this unique natural resource.

I offer these recipes as a starting point. They are not blueprints to be copied religiously but meant as an inspiration. Remember, times may vary depending on every input from your oven, pots, pans, freshness of ingredients and last but not least the weather.

Cooking is an act of sharing from the heart and I offer you some knowledge and wisdom I have collected along the way. I hope you enjoy stepping outside the square and learn to respect honey and its creators as I have. Be flexible, open-minded and most of all enjoy preparing, eating and sharing my cuisine.

maureen maxwell

■ I first met Maureen Maxwell when her wonderful Manuka Honey Vinegar was nominated for a New Zealand Honey Innovation Award in 2000, for which I was one of the judges. I remember being impressed by the amazing complexity, layers of flavour and long-lingering aftertaste.

I have worked with New Zealand honeys for many years, lecturing to chefs and food writers, holding honey classes and even presenting New Zealand honeys to the World Honey Congress in Vancouver. I have always promoted the fact that New Zealand has arguably the most diverse and wonderful selection of honeys in the world. I believe our honeys are worthy of the same sense of pride and recognition as our best wines; it is culinary pioneers like Maureen who are going to make that happen. This professional, sophisticated book, which clearly illustrates Maureen's passion for honey, is a wonderful start to a new way of seeing New Zealand honeys, both for New Zealanders and visitors to New Zealand.

bill floyd

sweet tips for honey

1 cup honey = 350 g
1 cup sugar = 250 g
1 tablespoon honey = 30 g

- Always store honey at room temperature. As honey matures, it naturally thickens or crystallises. If you wish to have it runny, remove the lid from the jar and place it in a bath of warm water or just heat it for a few seconds in the microwave. It is best stored out of direct sunlight in a well-sealed container.

- To measure honey, it is easiest using a spoon that has been dipped in hot water. Alternatively, spray or oil your measuring cup, and warm the honey to pour into it.

- When using honey as a substitute for sugar in cake recipes, use the same weight of honey as sugar but reduce the liquid by one-quarter.

- When baking, reduce the cooking temperature by 15ºC. Because of the fructose content, honey caramelises at a lower temperature than sugar.

- Be aware of the different flavours of honey. Generally speaking, the darker the honey the stronger the flavour.

- In recipes calling for white sugar, try substituting light honey; for recipes using golden syrup or treacle, use dark honey.

- To neutralise the honey's acidity, it is advisable to add $\frac{1}{2}$ teaspoon baking soda for each cup of honey used.

- To keep whipped cream firm, add a teaspoon of mild-flavoured honey during beating.

- Honey has nearly twice the energy value of sugar, i.e. it is nearly twice as sweet. If altering recipes, start by using 50 percent honey, e.g. $\frac{1}{2}$ cup sugar = 1 tablespoon honey and 2 tablespoons sugar.

- Take care when using honey in yeast recipes — the powerful antibacterial/antifungicidal properties can interfere with the yeast action. Use a mild honey or add when the fermentation is complete. Like sugar, honey can break down gluten, the protein necessary to hold bread dough together. Use strong flour for best results.

- When making yoghurt, the same applies. The antibacterial action usually inhibits the yeast culture. Add the honey when you are ready to serve.

- When next baking try adding 1–2 tablespoons of honey with the liquid ingredients. Your mix is more moist and will keep fresher for longer. Honey is hygroscopic. It attracts moisture; cakes will stay fresher, but biscuits may go soft and more chewy.

- For your lattés, a little honey will give your trim milk more volume.

- When heating honey always use a large pot and low heat. It will bubble and foam up dramatically as it heats, so watch carefully to avoid accidents.

- All honey is best stored below 20ºC in airtight containers out of direct sunlight.

honey types

Comb honey

This is cut directly from the hive with all the wax intact. For the beekeeper this is a rather wasteful way of harvesting honey because it takes the bee seven times more energy to produce wax than it does to produce honey. Commercial beekeepers prefer to give the extracted frames of beeswax back to the bees to refill with honey for next season: beeswax is the ultimate in recycled packaging.

Natural honey

This is honey as it is extracted from the hive. It is best not heated beyond hive temperature of 35ºC. Natural honey is filtered to remove impurities, some wax, propolis and pollen but otherwise left in its natural state. At first the honey is liquid. However, it will thicken and crystallise as it matures. Depending on the floral source this will offer a wide range of colour and texture. For liquid honey, gently warm in a water bath and stir to dissolve the crystals.

Creamed honey

This is attained by careful heating, filtering and stirring of the honey as it cools. A fine-grained starter honey is introduced and stirred through to encourage fine, smooth granulation to take place. Creamed honey is still all pure honey but just in another form.

Clear honey

All honey is liquid when it is first extracted, thickening as it matures. To remain clear and stable, honey is fine-filtered and pasteurised. Pasteurisation changes the molecular structure of the sugar in honey to slow granulation. It also inhibits bacterial and fungal growth, thereby improving the potential shelf life. Certain nutritional properties and some flavours are compromised with pasteurisation, so clear honey is more suited to mild commercial blends.

a spoonful of honey tasting notes

The question most commonly asked at honey tasting is, 'How do you control where the bees harvest?' Single-flower honey is the result of diligent work patterns on the part of the bees and watchful harvesting by the beekeeper. The bees follow the nectar flow and in turn this dictates the honey flow. The colony is a very efficient workforce which systemically harvests from the best flower source within its flight range, working until it exhausts this resource before moving on to the next flower type.

As different plants flower at different times, bees migrate to the flowers that provide the most abundant supply closest to their hive. The manuka flowers in spring, pohutukawa around Christmas and clover, for example, is at its best after Christmas, in those warm late summer days.

Single-flower honey can first be identified by uniformity of colour within a honey frame, then by the texture and taste. Mixed coloured frames naturally go into multiflora blends. Colours can be scientifically graded and pollen checks, under the microscope, can be used to assist with grading. However, like wine, the final judge is the experienced palate. The honey connoisseur can revel in the complexities of flavour, each wholly dependent on the floral source, climate and location.

Each season, each region produces its own imprint. The honey becomes a statement of time and place encapsulated in wax — a miniature potted landscape. Close your eyes and take the time not only to smell, but to taste the flowers. Individual flowers produce honey with distinctly different characteristics, colour, texture, aroma, viscosity and, of course, flavour, which varies from plant to plant.

When tasting honey, it is best to work at an ambient temperature of between 15 and 20ºC. Keep the taste sample at around a quarter of a teaspoon so that you are not overwhelmed by the sweetness and can appreciate the complexities of tasting honey. First, note the colour. As a general rule, light honey is more mild in flavour, medium amber honey develops a fuller flavour and dark honey is strong and bold on the palate.

Secondly, note the aroma from the jar, then pop a small amount of honey on the front of your tongue, let it dissolve, then roll the flavour around your mouth. Open your mouth and lick your lips and aerate the honey to release further flavours. Note the texture and search for flavours to clarify your perception. As it moves over your tongue the flavours develop. Take note of the aftertaste also.

If tasting several honeys, use warm black tea to cleanse the palate between samples. Take time to clear between different flavours. If you are arranging a 'tasting', try to provide a range of colours and flavours. Floral, herbal or tree honey all have different flavour dimensions. Or try single honey, e.g., clover in four different ways: comb, natural and extracted but not heat treated; creamed; and then pasteurised. Feel the response of your senses to each sample and compare the results.

With my experience in the wine industry, I often liken honey to wine: a manuka is herbaceous and tannic, like a powerful full-bodied dry red and a pohutukawa, with its floral sweeter notes is like a fruity dessert wine. Taste is very much down to personal preference, but I'm enjoying the taste journey and have included some tasting notes to guide you on your way. Enjoy! It's not often that something that tastes this good is also good for you.

For culinary purposes honey can be best grouped into three types: **sheer**, **mellow** and **strong**.

Sheer honeys

These are light in colour and delicate in flavour. Use them for delicate sauces, light dressings, baking and in desserts. These blend well with chocolate, especially white, cream and feminine flavours like rose petals, lemon verbena, balm, geranium, ground almonds, vanilla and spearmint.

Honey examples: Clover, Blue Borage and Thistle.

Mellow honeys

With these honeys the flavour is more developed and they have their own distinct characteristics. Mellow honeys are useful in heavier sauces, butter spreads and as toppings. They will also add distinct flavours to ice creams and sabayons. For complementary flavours they are best enhanced by floral or fruity essences — lavender, berry and peach notes or liqueurs all fit happily in this category.

Honey examples: Pohutukawa, Tawari, Rata, Wildflower and Farmhouse blends of Clover, Dandelion, Honeysuckle and Lotus Major.

Strong honeys

These are darker in colour, pungent and bold in both flavour and aroma and must be used with more care so that they do not overpower a dish. They are excellent for marinades, herbal dressings, savoury dishes, beef, game, spicy fish, and dipping sauces. Their texture tends to be more thixotropic or viscous. Complementary seasonings include garlic, chilli, ginger, star anise, thyme, rosemary, coriander, lemon grass and citrus.

Honey examples: Bush Honey blends, Manuka, Kanuka, Rewarewa, Thyme, Honeydew and Kamahi.

Main New Zealand honey varietal tasting notes

Sheer honeys

Clover

Our most abundant commercial honey crop, gathered from the vast pastoral farming areas, is mild, sweet and well rounded. Light amber in colour, it is readily available in creamed, liquid or comb form. A great introductory honey.

Blue Borage

Blue Borage (Viper's Bugloss or Patterson's Curse in Australia and Blueweed in the US). A light amber liquid honey with a nice chewy texture, mild in flavour, often with late summer-fresh hay or delicate rose flavours. The bees forage from the wild borage in the southern hill country.

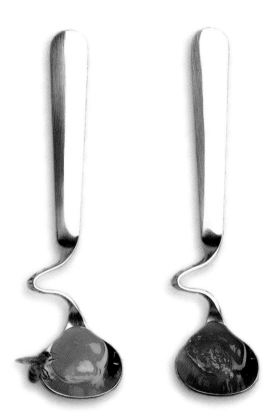

Thistle

Thistle, although a farmer's curse, is most welcomed by beekeepers because it produces a fine-textured white honey of delicate flavours. The best thistle honeys come from the South Island, from Canterbury through to Central Otago.

Mellow honeys

Pohutukawa

Pohutukawa flowers along the northern coastlines around Christmas with a halo of red flowers. The nectar produces a very white, sweet and strongly fragranced honey. Pohutukawa honey crystallises very rapidly with a coarse texture so it is best creamed as soon as it is extracted: a luscious and memorable honey that sometimes has a hint of salt.

Rata

The rata tree flowers in both islands with bright scarlet flowers. The honey is water white when first extracted and, like the pohutukawa, is best creamed to a pale, luscious, rich, yet not too sweet honey of distinct flavour. A connoisseur's honey in the mellow culinary range.

Tawari

A very elegant native tree with waxy white flowers. This is a honey with buttery yet fresh flavour; a creamy melt-in-the-mouth quality, lovely for desserts. It is best eaten fairly fresh, as it tends to have a high moisture content so is not a long keeper. Sheer to mellow depending on the season.

Wildflower
A romantic multifloral blend, which can include everything from bush to pastoral farmland.

Farmhouse Blend
Multifloral bush including pohutukawa and kowhai, depending on the season. A complex flavour but not as sweet as straight pohutukawa.

Bush
This honey has a multifloral blend of intense, strong, dark-flavoured bush honeys. They are thick and not so sweet so are best used for savoury dishes, sauces and marinades.

Strong honeys

Honeydew
This is unique in New Zealand in that it is not produced directly from plant nectar but from the excreta of insects that feed on the sap of the South Island beech trees. It is dark, slightly mineral in character and has hints of caramel.

Kamahi
Native kamahi trees are found throughout New Zealand and have long white flowers from November to January. The honey is pale gold but very strong in flavour. Earthy and bitter caramel on the back palate. Useful for marinades and savoury dishes.

Manuka
Rich amber in colour, intensely strong and earthy in flavour and aroma, mineral and herbaceous, sometimes there is an oily quality to Manuka honey. It is highly thixotropic and if blended with flowers from its tall cousin the kanuka tree, it granulates readily. Its antibacterial and antifungal properties make this an excellent soothing honey for use in hot drinks, savoury applications and with herbs and spices.

Manuka UMF Factor
The UMF or Unique Manuka Factor is a scientific grading method by which to measure the extra medicinal properties that some manuka honeys can possess. A greater than 10 rating ensures significant levels of valuable antibiotic, antifungal and antibacterial properties. This honey can be used both internally and externally for natural health purposes.

Thyme
In New Zealand the best thyme honey comes from the dry Otago hillsides where thymes grow wild. The resultant honey is strong, bold and pungent. Very herbal, both on the nose and palate, it is a wonderful honey to use with those herbaceous Mediterranean recipes.

Rewarewa
The New Zealand honeysuckle is related to the Australian bottlebrush. Unfortunately, the supply of Rewarewa varies from year to year and is not always available. Medium to dark amber in colour with a distinctive slightly burnt caramel finish, heavy-bodied and coarse-grained, its palm-sugary taste blends well with Asian and savoury dishes.

honey special ingredients notes

Standard New Zealand measurements are used in all recipes:
1 cup = 250 ml
1 tablespoon = 15 ml
1 teaspoon = 5 ml

Should you be unable to obtain BeesOnline products, see the website (www.beesonline.co.nz) for suppliers.
Substitutes can be used:

BeesOnline Manuka Honey Syrup
See page 98 for substitute suggestions.

Chilli Honey
Heat Bush Honey to 70ºC and infuse fresh chillies with the honey to taste — approximately 3–4 Jalapeno chillis to 250 ml honey. Chillies can be candied by blanching, seeding and placing in Bush Honey, then reducing until thick and almost caramelised.

Honeyed Ginger
At BeesOnline we pack jars of honey-crystallised stem ginger in liquid Bush Honey. Alternatively use stem ginger drained of sugar syrup then coated with honey.

Honeygar
Choose a naturally fermented wine vinegar and blend 1 tablespoon honey to 1 cup vinegar.

Roasted Honey Nuts
Freshly roast unsalted whole nuts and cover with pasteurised Bush Honey.

Rose Honey
A substitute for BeesOnline Rose Honey can be made by adding 1 geranium leaf to 1 cup Farmhouse Honey and gently warming to 70ºC. Hold for 5 minutes, then strain and bottle.

New Zealand native ingredients:

Horopito (Bush Pepper)
The leaves of an indigenous pepper tree found in the mountainous regions of the New Zealand bush.

Karengo
Hand-harvested and sun-dried seaweed gathered from New Zealand's unpolluted coastal waters, Karengo can be used refreshed, dried or oven crisp. It is a healthy and nourishing addition to the menu.

Kawakawa (Peppery Bush Basil)
The leaf of the kawakawa, a New Zealand native coastal shrub, can be used in both fresh and dried form. It can be used for both medicinal and culinary purposes.

Kelp Seasoning
Developed from hand-harvested and sun-dried kelp this is an excellent healthy earthy flavour alternative to salt.

Piko Piko
These are New Zealand edible fern shoots,which are nutty in flavour. Use and prepare like young asparagus spears.

For more information on indigenous herbs email karoo@xtra.co.nz

a honey of a **breakfast**

BeesOnline bircher muesli

The new BeesOnline Honey Centre Café sits on the trail for fishermen, surfers, mountain- and motorbikers, golfers and the horse brigade, to name a few of our early morning visitors. This muesli has its own fan club ...

325 g rolled oats
125 g coarse ground organic
   mixed nuts
3 apples, peeled and coarsely
   grated
500 ml fresh orange juice
100 g mixed dried fruit
   (sultanas, apricots, dates, etc.)
150 g BeesOnline Farmhouse
   Blend Honey

Mix all the ingredients together and do not use for at least 24 hours.

100 ml lightly whipped cream
150 g natural organic yoghurt
300 g fresh seasonal fruit

Combine these ingredients with 500 g of the base recipe as required. Serve with BeesOnline Manuka Honey Syrup and enjoy!

Chef's note: If you do not have BeesOnline Manuka Honey Syrup on hand, a little warmed honey of your choice could be substituted.

roasted pumpkin and honey nut dip

The first time I tried this recipe I had a house full of teenagers who devoured it ... even the boys!

800 g pumpkin, peeled, seeded and cut into 3 cm dice
1 tablespoon ground cumin
1 tablespoon ground coriander
5 tablespoons olive oil
2 tablespoons honey (dark Bush Honey or other strong-flavoured honey)
2 tablespoons Roasted Honey Nuts (see page 17)
salt and freshly ground black pepper
1–2 tablespoons BeesOnline Red Wine and Manuka Honeygar

Preheat the oven to 190°C. Put the pumpkin, spices and oil into a roasting dish and mix well. Roast until the pumpkin is soft and browned. Purée in a food processor or stick blender with the honey and nuts. Season with salt and pepper. Adjust consistency and taste with Honeygar.

Put some of this aside for a sandwich base.

Chef's notes: Often it is easier to cook the pumpkin with the skin on than remove the flesh. If you are softening the pumpkin in the microwave, pierce the skin well before cooking or it will explode. Serve warm or cold with warm pita bread or crusty French bread. Variations could include ginger or use BeesOnline Chilli Honey (see page 17).

Fairhall cucumber and melon soup

2 ripe honeydew melons
(skinned and seeded)

2 telegraph cucumbers

8 tips mint

4 tablespoons honey

3 cups yoghurt

1 cup freshly squeezed
orange juice

Place the melon, cucumber and mint in blender and blend until very smooth. Fold in the honey, yoghurt and orange juice. Decorate with melon balls and local seasonal fruits.

SERVES 4–6.

butternut squash soup

Pumpkin soup would have to be one of New Zealand's super comfort foods.

2 tablespoons butter

1 onion, chopped

2 cloves of garlic, minced

3 carrots, diced

1 stick celery

1 potato, peeled and diced

1 butternut squash, peeled,
seeded and diced

3 cups chicken or vegetable
stock

$\frac{1}{2}$ cup honey

1 teaspoon fresh thyme leaves,
crushed or $\frac{1}{4}$ teaspoon
dried thyme

salt and freshly ground black
pepper to taste

In a large pot, melt the butter over medium heat, then stir in the onion and garlic. Cook and stir until lightly browned, about 5 minutes. Stir in the carrots and celery. Cook and stir until tender, about 5 minutes. Stir in the potato, squash, stock, honey and thyme. Bring the mixture to the boil, reduce heat and simmer for 30–45 minutes or until the vegetables are tender. Remove from the heat and cool slightly. Transfer the mixture to a blender or food processor and process until smooth. Return the puréed soup to the pot. Season to taste with salt and pepper. Heat until hot and serve.

Chef's note: Pumpkin or pumpkin and kumara soup will take many different flavours. Add orange juice and a little zest, or try root ginger, coriander, cumin and nutmeg.

SERVES 6.

Jure's chilled grapefruit soup

Jure learnt this recipe from Nick Huffman during his time at Huka Lodge. A refreshing, different, yet elegant start to a meal.

250 ml fresh grapefruit juice
25 ml dry Martini Vermouth
10 ml Grenadine
50 ml mild honey, melted
Angostura bitters to taste

360 ml Sugar Syrup
(1 cup water, 1 cup sugar)
600 ml fresh grapefruit juice,
preferably pink
sprig of mint to garnish

Blend all ingredients well, then chill.

Serve in chilled bowls with a ball of sorbet in the centre. Garnish with a sprig of mint.

For sorbet
To make the sorbet, first make the Sugar Syrup by bringing the water and sugar to the boil. Cool, then chill. Blend with the grapefruit juice and freeze. When half frozen, gently break it up with a whisk then continue freezing until firm. Alternatively use your ice-cream maker.

SERVES 2.

hot roasted garlic and chilli honey spread

garlic bulbs
olive oil
1–2 teaspoons Chilli Honey (see page 17 or chef's note below)
red chilli, finely shredded

Select whole firm garlic heads. Rub off any excess papery skin from the outside. Carefully slice the top off the entire head of garlic exposing tops of cloves through to the core. Nestle the bulb loosely in tinfoil and drizzle a little olive oil over the top. Bake in a moderate oven (180°C) for about 40–50 minutes until soft. Take from the oven and pour Chilli Honey over and some finely shredded red chilli. Serve warm.

To eat, squish out roasted garlic paste with side of a knife, blend with Chilli Honey and spread on warm crispy bread. Freshly ground salt and/or a squeeze of lemon could be interesting side extras.

Chef's note: If you do not have BeesOnline Chilli Honey in your pantry, blanch 1 or 2 red chillis to taste, and infuse with 1 cup of bush honey, warming to 70°C and holding for 5 minutes. Cool and bottle.

caponata

Anna Tasca Lanza in Sicily tells me that caponata is only narrowly beaten into second place as the national dish of Sicily by pasta con le sarde (pasta served with sardines and tomato sauce). I have sampled many fine examples of caponata. Anna often served it garnished with orange slices, fresh basil or marinated baby octopus. I will share with you the recipe given to me by an elegant Sicilian, Eleonora Consoli, who has written several books and heads a wonderful commercial kitchen and cookery school called Cucina de Sole.

1 large long purple aubergine
salt
extra virgin olive oil
2 sticks celery, blanched and sliced in long diagonal pieces
2 green capsicums, sliced
1 medium onion, finely diced
1 anchovy fillet
1 tablespoon tomato paste
1–2 tablespoons strong-flavoured honey
1 small cup (or wine glass full, as Anna described) of red wine vinegar (optional)
2–3 tablespoons raisins (or currants)
2–3 tablespoons diced green olives
pine nuts and capers to taste (optional)
freshly ground black pepper
3 hard-boiled free-range eggs

Slice the aubergine lengthwise, salt and rest for 20 minutes. Rinse and pat dry. Fry in a little extra virgin olive oil, being careful not to get the oil too hot, as this will taint the flavour. Continue to sauté until golden, then lift out into a mixing bowl. Do the same with the celery and then the capsicum and onion. It is best to cook each vegetable separately, as the cooking times are quite different. In a just-warm pan melt the anchovy fillet, stir in the tomato paste, then the honey and vinegar. Pour over the vegetables and add the dried fruit, olives, (and nuts and capers if using) and mix thoroughly. Season with salt and pepper. If too stiff add a little water. Form into a pyramid on a flat serving dish and garnish with hard-boiled eggs, cut in half lengthwise. Serve cool.

SERVES 6.

pacific rim emu marinated in red wine and manuka honeygar and garnished with piko piko (New Zealand fern shoot)

1 strip emu fillet, approximately 400–500 g, skinned and de-sinewed

Kinaki Wild Herb Baste, approximately 1 level teaspoon

1 tablespoon olive oil

1 teaspoon sesame oil

ice cubes to chill

SAUCE

¼ cup soy sauce

1 tablespoon Bush Blend honey, warmed

2 tablespoons finely chopped root ginger

1 tablespoon very finely chopped garlic

piko piko shoots (see page 17)

clarified butter

1 tablespoon BeesOnline Red Wine and Manuka Honeygar

Lightly slash criss-cross patterns on each side of meat. Rub in Kinaki Wild Herb Baste.

Combine all the sauce ingredients and reserve half. Pour remaining sauce over the meat. Leave to stand for 5–10 minutes. Lift the meat from the sauce and pat dry. Heat the olive and sesame oil in a pan and when very hot quickly brown the meat on all sides. Remove the meat from the pan, loosely wrap in foil and immediately cover with ice to prevent further cooking. Once the meat is cool, remove the ice and freeze for about 1 hour to firm for easy slicing.

To serve: Slice the meat paper-thin (preferably with a bacon slicer) and arrange on a platter or croutes. Mix 1 tablespoon of Red Honeygar with 1 tablespoon of reserved sauce and serve in a dipping bowl or drizzle over the canapés. Wash and trim the piko piko shoots. Sauté briefly in clarified butter and drizzle with the Honeygar. Use as a garnish.

Chef's notes: Asian bean-thread vermicelli can be used as a garnish either deep fried or just boiled in green tea. Kinaki Wild Herb Baste is available from Maorifood.com or (09) 415 9658.

SERVES 2.

honey mustard glazed bacon and scallop bites

Excellent with Christmas cocktails or as an addition to the Christmas barbecue.

16 scallops
8 rashers of rindless middle bacon
BeesOnline Honey Mustard
presoaked toothpicks or satay sticks

Place a scallop on a bacon strip, spread a little Honey Mustard on either side, roll up and secure with a damp toothpick or satay stick.

VARIATIONS

This treatment is equally good with sausages, mushrooms or small pieces of banana.If you run out of BeesOnline Honey Mustard, make up a sauce using 3 tablespoons honey to 1 tablespoon soy sauce and brush over the scallops. Wrap up in bacon and cook to taste.

SERVES 6.

Chef's note: Presoak your wooden skewers in water to stop them burning on the barbecue.

pipi, kumara and phyllo canapés

½ bucket fresh pipis
2 tablespoons BeesOnline White
    Wine and Clover Honeygar
phyllo pastry
2 tablespoons melted butter
2 tablespoons olive oil
2 scrubbed kumara
knob of butter
2 cm root ginger, finely grated
salt and freshly ground
    black pepper
1 egg yolk
¼ teaspoon Kinaki ground
    kawakawa (see page 17)
watercress to garnish

Scrub the pipi and steam open over a little water. When opened, remove from their shells and put into Honeygar to marinade. Layer 4 sheets of phyllo, brushing in between with combined melted butter and olive oil. Using kitchen scissors, trim into small squares and line miniature muffin pans, pleating in gently as you go. Boil or microwave the kumara until it is tender. Mash with the butter, ginger, salt and pepper, egg yolk and a little milk if necessary to make a smooth 'Duchesse' of piping consistency. Season with kawakawa. Pipe Duchesse into phyllo cases. Bake at 200ºC until golden. Place the pipi on top of the pastry cases. Garnish with watercress.

SERVES 12 AS FINGER FOOD.

kina mousse

BeesOnline Café won 'Best Individual Beer and Food Match' in the Monteith's Wild Food Challenge with this recipe. 'Kina have a beer with that?' matched with Monteith's Black Beer.

fresh ginger, a thumb-sized piece, peeled and finely sliced

1 medium onion, chopped

2 garlic cloves, minced

4 sprigs fresh coriander, roughly chopped, keeping leaf separate

olive oil

500 g kina, fresh or frozen (from any good fish market)

150 ml cream

100 g BeesOnline Honeyed Ginger (see page 17)

300 g butter, diced into 2 cm cubes

salt, freshly ground pepper and kelp seasoning

Sauté the ginger, onion, garlic and coriander roots and stem in a little olive oil. Add the kina then the cream. Reduce by half. Remove the kina to a food processor with Honeyed Ginger and coriander leaf. Reduce the remaining liquid again by half, then add to the food processor. Whiz, adding butter one cube at a time until all is absorbed. This takes about 3 minutes. Season to taste with salt, freshly ground pepper and kelp seasoning.

SERVES 6.

Chef's note: For the competition we served two quenelles (egg-shaped servings, formed using 2 dessertspoons) of mousse on mussel shells. A third shell with Red Wine and Manuka Honeygar nestled on a bed of crispy fried karengo (edible New Zealand harvested seaweed). Korus of Flaxseed and Beer Bread completed the ensemble with a wee drizzle of flaxseed oil (very high source of Omega 3) and reduced Honeygar to finish. Honeyed Ginger could be replaced with stem ginger covered in warmed Bush Honey. For Honeygar substitute a good-quality red wine or light balsamic vinegar.

phyllo fish fingers with avocado, wasabi and kiwi fruit dipping sauce

These are great for cocktail parties, or you can make larger parcels for a main course.

olive oil
600 g fresh fish fillets (e.g. gurnard)
1 teaspoon prepared wasabi paste
phyllo pastry
sesame seeds

DIPPING SAUCE

1 avocado
3 kiwi fruit
$\frac{1}{2}$ teaspoon finely grated root ginger
1 tablespoon warmed strong honey (Bush Blend or Manuka)
1 teaspoon chilli sauce
salt and freshly ground black pepper
$\frac{1}{2}$ teaspoon wasabi paste

Heat a little oil in a frying pan and pan-fry the fish until it is just cooked. Cool and spread with wasabi paste. Cut into finger-sized pieces. Take a sheet of phyllo pastry, lightly brush with oil and fold into three widthwise. Wrap the fish fingers into long rolls, then place on a baking sheet, with the fold underneath. Brush with a little oil and sprinkle with sesame seeds. Repeat until all the fish is used. Bake at 200ºC until golden, approximately 10 minutes.

To make the dipping sauce, put all ingredients in a food processor and blend until smooth. Serve alongside hot phyllo fingers.

SERVES 12 AS FINGER FOOD.

smoked salmon and baby ricotta pikelets

The delicate flavours of egg and smoked salmon are well suited to dry-style Champagne or méthode traditionelle. These pikelets are great for entertaining or you could do larger 'hotcakes' for an elegant brunch dish.

200 g ricotta
1 egg
1 cup self-raising flour, sifted
½ teaspoon salt
1 cup milk
2 tablespoons butter, melted
1 tablespoon butter to fry

Beat together the ricotta and egg. Stir in the flour, salt, milk and first measure of butter. Allow to rest for 5–10 minutes. Fry the pikelets in butter by the heaped teaspoonful until lightly golden on each side. Cool on a wire rack so they do not steam and become soggy. (The pikelets can be frozen on a tray at this stage and then put into snap-lock bags for later use.) For larger pikelets, use a dessertspoon. Spread a little Herb Cream on each pikelet and top with a piece of smoked salmon. Sprinkle with cracked pepper and serve.

Herb cream
In a bowl or blender place the cream cheese, butter, honey, mustard, spring onion, dill and lemon zest, and mix well.

½ cup cream cheese
75 g butter, softened
2 teaspoons honey (Bush Blend)
2 teaspoons wholegrain mustard
1 spring onion, finely sliced
1 teaspoon chopped dill
grated rind ½ lemon

500 g smoked salmon, sliced
cracked pepper

MAKES 70 PIKELETS TO SERVE 35 AS HORS D'OEUVRE.

fresh grilled figs with candied chillies and prosciutto

We had a wonderful supply of fresh figs last autumn and at the time also had masses of organic chillies on hand ... hence a recipe was born.

4 Jalapeno chillies
½ cup Bush Honey
6–8 fresh figs
12 strips of prosciutto or bacon

Wash and seed the chillies. Blanch, then caramelise with Bush Honey until translucent and the honey has thickened. Watchful that the caramel does not burn, stir from time to time. Slice the figs in half, top with slivers of chilli, then wrap in prosciutto or bacon and grill till crispy. Serve warm.

oysters with chilli honey salsa

We often serve fresh oysters, either Bluff or local Kaipara in season, 'au naturel' just with a drizzle or dip of Honeygar. Fresh salsas are made up daily, varying ingredients depending on the availability of fresh ingredients.

CHILLI HONEY SALSA

½ **red capsicum, finely diced**

½ **yellow capsicum, finely diced**

¼ **telegraph cucumber, peeled, seeded and finely diced**

1 **clove garlic, minced finely in ¼ teaspoon sea salt**

2 **tablespoons finely sliced Honeyed Ginger (see page 17)**

1 **small fresh chilli, seeds removed and finely sliced**

75 **ml olive oil**

25 **ml Honeygar (see page 17)**

1 **tablespoon Chilli Honey (see page 17)**

salt and freshly ground black pepper

oysters

Combine all and season with salt and pepper to taste.

cucumber and radish salad with honey dressing

Over our first summer at the BeesOnline Café we served chunky Mussel Fish Cakes with this colourful salad.

1 large cucumber, peeled, seeded and finely sliced

1 bunch of red radishes, scrubbed and finely sliced

2 teaspoons honey (Bush Blend is best)

3 tablespoons olive oil

2 tablespoons Red Wine and Manuka Honeygar

1 tablespoon lemon juice

1 $\frac{1}{2}$ teaspoons fresh dill, snipped with scissors

Salt the cucumber, allow to stand for approximately 1 hour, then discard the liquid. Mix with the radish. Blend the remaining ingredients together and toss through the salad. Sprinkle with dill.

SERVES 4.

watermelon, honeyed ginger and grapefruit salad

This combination is light and spicy for a refreshing summer treat.

**2 cups peeled, diced and seeded
   watermelon flesh**
**2 grapefruit (Ruby or Pink create
   a great colour)**
**BeesOnline Honeyed Ginger
   to taste, approximately
   1–2 tablespoons**

Place the watermelon flesh in a bowl. With a sharp paring knife peel the grapefruit, removing all the white pith, then slice or, if preferred, carefully lift out the segments. Add with juice to the watermelon. Stir some Honeyed Ginger through the salad.

SERVES 4.

winter pear and bacon salad

Manuka honey lends a barley sugar flavour to this simple but stunning starter or light meal.

3 medium pears
12 strips bacon
¼ cup Manuka Honey
1 teaspoon five-spice powder
**1 teaspoon grated fresh
   ginger root**
½ cup ginger wine
salad greens for garnish

Recipe courtesy of
NZ House and Garden magazine

Preheat oven to 180ºC. Cut the pears into quarters and remove the core. Wrap each piece with a bacon strip and place in a small, shallow baking dish. Combine the honey, five-spice powder and ginger and brush over pears. Pour over the ginger wine and bake for 10–12 minutes until the bacon is crisp and the pears are tender. Serve on warmed plates, garnished with salad greens.

SERVES 4.

Chef's note: Stone's Ginger Wine has been used. A dry sherry could be substituted with 2 teaspoons of finely chopped crystallised ginger added.

warm baby beetroot and orange spice salad

Here's a fabulously colourful winter salad to tempt the palate. I have used a few bright calendula petals from the garden to finish this dish.

18 whole baby beetroot (freshly cooked or tinned)
4 sweet oranges
1 small red onion
$\frac{1}{2}$ cup olive oil
$\frac{1}{4}$ cup reserved beetroot liquid
3 tablespoons red wine vinegar
1 teaspoon five-spice powder
1 tablespoon runny honey (try our BeesOnline Bush Blend Honey)
sea salt and cracked pepper
calendula petals if available

Drain and halve the beetroot, reserving $\frac{1}{4}$ cup liquid. Peel the oranges, removing white pith, and cut into thick slices. Slice the red onion thinly. Layer the beetroot, oranges and red onion in a shallow dish. Place the olive oil, beetroot liquid, vinegar, five-spice powder, honey and salt and pepper in a screw-top jar and shake well. Pour the dressing over the salad and leave to marinate for at least 30 minutes. Cover the dish and microwave for 2–3 minutes to warm through, or warm in a saucepan. Serve in small bowls or on a bed of fresh greens drizzled with the dressing. Toss a few calendula petals on the top for a garnish.

SERVES 6.

Chef's note: Try using Red Wine and Manuka Honeygar for this dressing.

honey-roasted chestnuts with button onions, crispy bacon and parsnip wafers

I thought this might be fun for all those midwinter Christmas parties!

2 tablespoons Chestnut Honey
  or other strong-flavoured
  honey
2 tablespoons wholegrain
  mustard
¼ cup olive oil
chestnuts, peeled
button onions, peeled
parsnips, peeled and sliced
bacon cut into 2 cm-sized pieces
salt and freshly ground
  black pepper

Warm the honey and mustard together (this can be done in the microwave). Stir in the olive oil. Oil the base of a roasting tin and preheat the oven to 200ºC. Toss the vegetables, then pour over honey, mustard and oil mix. Stir to coat vegetables. After 10 minutes, turn the vegetables then put the bacon on top and cook until golden. Season with salt and pepper and serve.

SERVES 4.

smoked chicken and prosciutto salad

This combination is light and spicy for a refreshing summer treat.

6 slices prosciutto (or bacon)

250 g smoked chicken

2 large fresh peaches, peeled or sliced

¼ cup seedless sliced green grapes or 1 sliced kiwi fruit

150 g feta cheese, diced

1 small–medium onion, finely sliced (red onion adds great colour)

1 medium cos lettuce

DRESSING

200 g low-fat natural yoghurt

¼ cup lemon juice

1 tablespoon Honey Mustard

1 clove garlic crushed in ¼ teaspoon natural salt

freshly ground black pepper

Grill the prosciutto (or bacon) until crisp. Cool and crumble into bite-sized pieces. Shred the chicken into salad-sized pieces. Whisk the dressing ingredients together and toss with the prepared fruit, chicken, cheese and onion. Wash the lettuce, place on a serving plate and pile salad on top. Garnish with crisp prosciutto. Serve with fresh warm bread.

SERVES 2.

Chef's note: This also makes a great salad sandwich filling.

green beans with honey and garlic

Oriental-style beans go well with a smart fillet steak main course. I used Avocado Honey here, but a strong Bush Blend, Chestnut or Manuka would be good with this recipe.

French beans, freshly picked,
  washed and trimmed
1 tablespoon olive oil
2 cloves garlic, finely chopped
1–2 teaspoons strong honey

Sauté the beans quickly in the olive oil over a high heat, tossing all the time for 1–2 minutes. Add the garlic and honey, toss for 1 more minute and serve immediately. The beans should still be a little crisp, bright green and glossy.

SERVES 2–4.

honey-roasted tomatoes

We use these all the time at the Café — they're intense in colour and flavour.

6 large tomatoes (plum-shaped
  Roma look and taste great)
salt and kelp seasoning
freshly ground black pepper
fresh thyme
1–2 tablespoons strong honey,
  warmed
olive oil to sprinkle

Preheat the oven to 150ºC. Core and cut the tomatoes in half. Place cut-side up in a shallow roasting tray, either non-stick or lined with baking paper. Season with salt, kelp seasoning, pepper and sprigs of fresh thyme, then drizzle a little warm honey over, then a little olive oil. Bake until the tomatoes are slightly shrivelled and rich in flavour and colour. They're great as a side dish hot or cold.

Chef's note: Chilli Honey would be great used here. If you do not have any, try very finely chopping a fresh chilli and sprinkling over tomatoes before the honey.

SERVES 6.

baked honey mustard potatoes

1 kg potatoes
salt and freshly ground black
    pepper
1 cup milk
a few onion slices
1 cut clove garlic
1 egg, beaten
1 tablespoon BeesOnline
    Honey Mustard
4 tablespoons grated
    tasty cheese
butter

Slice the potatoes thinly (peel if liked), arrange in an ovenproof dish and sprinkle with salt and pepper. Warm the milk with the onion slices and garlic, strain, then combine with the beaten egg and Honey Mustard. Pour over the potatoes, sprinkle with cheese and dot with butter. Bake at 180ºC for about 45–50 minutes or until the potatoes are soft when tested with a skewer.

SERVES 4.

honeyed baby turnips with lemon thyme

500 g baby turnips
45 g butter
$\frac{1}{4}$ cup honey
3 teaspoons lemon juice
$\frac{1}{2}$ teaspoon lemon rind
    (grated or zest)
3 teaspoons chopped fresh
    lemon thyme leaves

Rinse and lightly scrub the turnips under water. Trim the tips and stalks. Cook in boiling water for 1 minute, then drain. Rinse under cold water and drain again. Heat the butter in a pan and add the honey. Bring to the boil, then add the lemon juice and rind.

Boil over a high heat for 3 minutes. Add the turnips to the mixture. Cook over high heat for a further 3 minutes or until the turnips are almost tender and well glazed (test with a skewer). Add the lemon thyme. Remove the pan from the heat and toss until the turnips are well coated. Serve warm.

SERVES 4 AS SIDE DISH.

Claudia Roden's honeyed aubergine

This recipe comes via Julie Biuso and is finger-licking good.

750 g (about 3 small) aubergines
salt
2–3 garlic cloves, crushed
sunflower oil for frying
5 cm piece ginger, grated, or
the juice squeezed out in
a garlic press
1 teaspoon ground cumin
large pinch cayenne or chilli
pepper, or to taste
5 tablespoons runny honey
juice of 1 lemon
5 tablespoons water

Remove the calyx and stem from each aubergine, then cut into 1 cm slices. Sprinkle generously with salt and leave in a colander for 1 hour to release their juices, then wash off the salt and dry with absorbent kitchen paper. Prepare the honey sauce. In a wide frying pan, fry the garlic in 2 tablespoons of oil for seconds only, stirring until the aroma rises, then take it off the heat; do not let it brown. Add the ginger, cumin, cayenne or chilli pepper, honey, lemon juice and about 5 tablespoons of water. Fry the aubergine slices in a separate frying pan in very hot oil, turning once, until they are lightly browned. They do not need to be thoroughly cooked as they will cook further in the sauce. Drain on absorbent kitchen paper and gently press more paper on top to remove as much oil as possible. Now cook the aubergine slices in the honey sauce over a low heat, either in batches so that they are in one layer, or put them all in together and rearrange them so that each gets some cooking in the sauce. Cook for about 10 minutes or until the slices have absorbed the sauce and become soft. Add a little water if necessary.

Let cool and serve cold or at room temperature with bread.

SERVES 6–8.

How to oven-bake aubergine:

Fried aubergine is rich and delicious to eat, but it has a bad habit of soaking up too much oil. If the aubergine is to be incorporated into other dishes, or when you want a less rich dish, it can be brushed with olive oil and oven baked. This uses much less oil than frying and ensures that the dish it is incorporated into does not become excessively rich and oily. Slice the eggplant into rounds and brush both sides with olive oil. Lay the slices flat in one layer on a baking tray (line the tray with a Teflon sheet if you have one). Bake for about 20 minutes, or until tender and brown, in an oven preheated to 180ºC. Use immediately, or cool, refrigerate and use within 24 hours.

honey-candied cherry tomatoes

While recently travelling in Italy, I enjoyed a pleasant evening sharing food ideas and tastes around the table with an inspiring chef called Corrado Assenza. Corrado runs a traditional bakery and café in Noto. Tradition and food purity are at the core of his culinary adventures.

When I asked him about the candied tomatoes (which he served alongside a fresh marmalade with ricotta cheese), he began by explaining how important it was to source the right tomatoes, and the perfect location in which to grow them . . . the quality of the ingredients being more important than the recipe!

cherry tomatoes, sun ripened
warmed light amber honey to
 cover, medium flavour range,
 such as Bush Blend
good pinch fresh chilli powder
fresh cheese to serve
freshly ground black pepper

Peel the tomatoes by carefully removing the core with a small sharp knife, plunging them into boiling water then into chilled water, then peeling off the skin. Place in a clean sterilised glass jar. Warm the honey with the chilli powder. Pour over the tomatoes and seal.

Serve with cheese and finish with a grind of black pepper.

Chef's note: I like to include 2 or 3 fresh chillis in each jar instead of using dried chilli powder. I blanch the chillies in boiling water for 30 seconds, refresh in iced water then place in the jars with the tomatoes.

barbecued Middle Eastern-inspired aubergine

1 medium aubergine
100 ml olive oil
1 large clove garlic, peeled and finely chopped
3 tablespoons strong-flavoured honey (Manuka, Bush Blend or Chestnut)
1 teaspoon ground paprika
1 teaspoon ground coriander
¼ teaspoon cayenne pepper
1 teaspoon cumin seeds
sea salt and freshly ground black pepper to taste
2 tablespoons Red Wine and Manuka Honeygar

Slice the aubergine into 1 cm rounds. Combine the olive oil, garlic, honey, paprika, ground coriander, cayenne pepper, cumin seeds, salt and pepper in a small saucepan or microwave bowl. Bring the mixture gently to the boil, stirring, then simmer for 2 minutes. Brush the marinade over the aubergine slices, then grill until golden. Turn slices over, brush with remaining marinade and grill. Sprinkle cooked aubergine with Honeygar. Serve warm or at room temperature.

Chef's note: This glaze could be used on other vegetables like thick slices of precooked kumara, or try it as a baste for chicken or fish.

SERVES 4.

courgettes with honey sauce

I received this recipe from Eleonora Consoli in Sicily. The Sicilians have their own wonderful regional cuisine, which tastes of its history: at some time Sicily has been owned by the Greeks, Arabs and French and now Italy, so interesting sweet, sour and spicy flavours from these countries have come through.

600 g green courgettes
1 teaspoon salt
½ cup extra virgin olive oil
1 clove garlic
2 tablespoons red wine vinegar
1 tablespoon honey, strong Bush or Manuka Blend
freshly ground black pepper
a sprinkle of ground cinnamon
6–8 fresh basil leaves

Wash the courgettes, trim and slice lengthwise. Sprinkle with salt and let sit for 20 minutes. Rinse and dry with paper towels. Heat the olive oil in a frying pan until hot. Add the courgettes and cook until lightly browned. Drain and arrange in a serving dish.

In the same pan sauté the garlic briefly until golden. Turn off the heat and add the vinegar, honey and a dash of pepper. Reduce slightly, remove the garlic and pour over the courgettes. Sprinkle with a little pinch of cinnamon. Garnish with basil leaves and serve, either warm or cold.

Chef's note: The vinegar and honey could be replaced with 3 tablespoons BeesOnline Red Wine and Manuka Honeygar.

SERVES 6.

pickled honey mushrooms

2 tablespoons olive oil
500 g button mushrooms
12 whole garlic cloves, peeled
2 tablespoons Manuka Honey
2 tablespoons red wine vinegar
fresh thyme sprigs
cracked black pepper and Kelp
   Seasoning (see page 17),
   or salt

Heat the oil in a shallow frying pan and cook the mushrooms until coloured. Then add the garlic cloves and cook for 3 minutes. Add the honey and allow to simmer for a few minutes until they begin to caramelise. Add the vinegar, thyme and pepper. Cool before pouring into a sealed container. Store in the refrigerator.

This is excellent as a side dish, on an antipasto platter or served with bread and cheese.

Chef's note: Chef Charles Royal does something similar with mushrooms, garlic and honey. After caramelising the honey, he adds some of his fabulous Horopito Piri Piri Seasoning, then sour cream. Serve with crostini.

roasted carrots with red honeygar and mint

1.25 kg carrots (or parsnips or
   red capsicums), peeled and
   split into batons
olive oil
¼ cup BeesOnline Red Honeygar
⅓ cup finely chopped fresh
   mint leaves
freshly ground black pepper and
   salt to garnish

Heat oven to 180ºC. Toss the carrots in a large bowl with enough olive oil to coat, then roast in a single layer for approximately 30 minutes or until vegetables are soft and starting to brown on the edges. Drain on paper towels. Combine the vegetables, Honeygar and fresh mint. Season to taste with salt and pepper. Serve warm or at room temperature.

Chef's note: If you do not have Honeygar, use ¼ cup good quality red wine vinegar and add 2 teaspoons of strong honey.

SERVES 6 AS SIDE DISH.

honeyed stir-fried vegetables

750 g mixed vegetables, sliced,
   or cut into small pieces
   (e.g. snow peas, beans,
   carrot sticks, broccoli or
   cauliflower florets, asparagus
   spears, sliced capsicum)
1 teaspoon sesame oil
1 teaspoon sesame seeds
2 teaspoons honey
¼ teaspoon grated fresh ginger

Blanch the vegetables by popping them into boiling water for 1 minute, then drain immediately and refresh in cold water to stop cooking and set colour. Drain thoroughly.

When ready to serve, heat the sesame oil and sesame seeds in a wok, add the vegetables, honey and ginger and stir-fry until heated through.

SERVES 6.

BeesOnline honey-roasted vegetables

2 large onions, quartered
6 medium carrots, chopped into
   chunky pieces
2 medium kumara, peeled and
   cut into wedges
⅓ cup olive oil
60 g butter, melted
2 tablespoons strong-flavoured
   honey
1 tablespoon wholegrain
   mustard
1 tablespoon sesame seeds

Combine the vegetables in a large roasting tin and drizzle with half the olive oil. Bake, uncovered, at 180ºC for an hour or until the vegetables are just tender. Combine the butter with the remaining oil, honey and mustard, and pour over vegetables in dish. Bake for a further 20–30 minutes or until the vegetables are soft and the glaze is slightly thickened. Sesame seeds are best sprinkled on about 15 minutes before the end of cooking.

SERVES 6.

Chef's note: I use lots of different vegetables this way. Baby turnips, parsnips, potatoes and slices of capsicum added near the end of cooking add variety and colour. Whole nuts, especially macadamias, are delicious added in the last 15 minutes. It makes a good hot dish for vegetarians.

marinated celery, fennel and onion with lemon yoghurt

Inspired by the classic French dish, 'Vegetables à la Grecque', these crisp, tangy, marinated vegetables make a wonderful meze served on their own, accompanied by the lemon yoghurt, or with an array of other dishes.

300 g cauliflower (about ¼ head) divided into florets
300 g fennel (about 1 bulb), trimmed and cut into thin wedges
1 heart celery, trimmed and cut into 2 cm pieces, leaves reserved for garnish
2 Spanish onions, cut into thin wedges
½ cup extra virgin olive oil
3 cloves garlic, bruised
1 ½ tablespoons coriander seeds, lightly crushed
3 dried bay leaves
4 one cm-wide strips of lemon rind
1 tablespoon Bush Blend Honey
200 ml white wine vinegar
500 ml dry white wine

LEMON YOGHURT
1 cup Greek-style yoghurt
1 tablespoon finely grated lemon rind
¼ cup extra virgin olive oil
sea salt and freshly ground black pepper

For Lemon Yoghurt, combine all ingredients in a bowl, season to taste with salt and pepper and stir until smooth. Refrigerate until required.

Blanch the vegetables separately in boiling salted water for 1 minute, then plunge into iced water. Drain well. Heat the olive oil in a large saucepan, add the garlic, coriander seeds, bay leaves and lemon rind and stir over low heat for 5 minutes or until the mixture is fragrant. Add the honey, white wine vinegar and white wine, and cook on a low heat for 3 minutes. Remove from the heat, add the vegetables, stirring to coat, then cool to room temperature.

Serve the marinated vegetables at room temperature, with the Lemon Yoghurt passed around separately. Marinated vegetables will keep in an airtight container in the refrigerator for up to 3 days.

SERVES 6–8.

This recipe comes from the *Australian Gourmet Traveller*, September 2002.

mains

gingered honey steak and ale pie

When winter arrives and the fire is lit daily in our Café our specials turn to a richer fare. This dish is a favourite among our male customers. The recipe also works well with lamb or venison.

600 g lean beef
   (e.g. topside fillet)
1 tablespoon gingered honey
   (or ginger)
2 teaspoons chopped parsley
   and thyme
250 ml ale (Monteith's Black)
1 teaspoon tomato paste
salt and freshly ground
   black pepper
25 g flour
oil
2 large onions, chopped
10 g honey
500 ml beef stock or water
500 g puff or flaky pastry

EGG WASH
1 fresh egg beaten with
   2 tablespoons milk

Cut the beef into 2 cm cubes or strips. Mix the gingered honey, herbs, ale and tomato paste into a marinade. Pour over the beef and leave for 2 hours or overnight. Strain the beef, keeping the marinade to one side. Season the beef with salt and pepper and roll in the flour. Heat some oil in a frying pan and quickly colour the beef on both sides. Transfer to a casserole dish. Add the onions to the pan and fry to a light brown colour, then add to the ale marinade with the honey and sufficient beef stock to cover the meat. Cover with a tight-fitting lid and simmer gently in a moderate oven (150–180ºC) until meat is tender — approximately 2 hours. Skim the top and season to taste.

Roll pastry to 2 cm thickness. Cut squares right through 10 x 10 cm and cut inner lid square not quite through to base. Place on a baking tray, then glaze with Egg Wash. Bake until golden. Lift lid and hollow out. Discard extra pastry. Cool.

Warm pastry through and fill with warm beef to serve.

Chef's note: We make individual square vol-au-vent cases at the Café or you can make up your own pies. When using a tin I prefer to use shortcrust pastry on the bottom and flaky pastry for the top. The shortcrust creates a firmer, crisper base.

SERVES 4.

welsh lamb (cig oen a mel)

Back in the early 1980s I was working as a cook in the West Country in the United Kingdom. The housekeeper shared this wonderful recipe with me. Cider was then more readily available than wine.

1 shoulder or leg of lamb
2 cloves garlic
sea salt
freshly ground black pepper
125 g honey, Bush or Thyme
450 ml dry cider
1 teaspoon chopped mint
1 ½ teaspoons chopped fresh
   thyme, or ¼ teaspoon dried
25 g plain flour
juice of 1 lemon

Preheat oven to 230ºC. Line a roasting dish with a piece of foil large enough to wrap over the top of the joint. Cut small slits in the joint and insert slices of 1 clove garlic. Cut the second clove in half and rub all over the outside of the meat. Place the joint in the dish and season with salt and pepper. Mix the honey with 300 ml of cider and pour over the joint. Sprinkle with the herbs, cover with foil and cook in the preheated oven for 30 minutes. Open the foil and baste with the remaining cider. Close the foil again. Reduce the heat to 180ºC and cook for a further hour, folding back the foil for the last 30 minutes. Remove the meat and rest on a warmed serving dish while you skim the fat off, then make gravy with the pan juices, flour and season with lemon juice. Serve piping hot with the meat.

SERVES 4.

Thai-inspired rack of lamb with lime, mint and honey dressing and sweet cinnamon rice

4 cloves garlic, finely chopped
   and blended with ¼ cup olive oil
3 racks trimmed lamb
salt and freshly ground
   black pepper

DRESSING

1 stalk lemon grass, finely
   chopped
3 tablespoons Nam pla (Asian
   fish sauce)
2 teaspoons finely chopped garlic
2 tablespoons fresh mint
1 fresh chilli, seeded and finely
   chopped
3 tablespoons lime juice
1 tablespoon mild honey
6 tablespoons olive oil

RICE

4 tablespoons butter
½ cup finely diced celery
½ cup diced onion
½ cup diced carrots
½ cup yellow lentils
1 ½ cups long grain rice
½ teaspoon salt
4 cinnamon sticks
4 cups water
½ cup currants
3 cm piece root ginger, grated

(Wash the rice and lentils and soak them both in fresh water for 1 hour.)

Combine the garlic and olive oil. Rub over the lamb and season with salt and pepper. Combine all dressing ingredients well.

To prepare the rice, melt 2 tablespoons of butter, add the vegetables and sauté gently for 5 minutes. Add the lentils, rice, salt, cinnamon, water, currants and ginger. Bring to the boil. Keep the heat high and when the water has reduced to the level of the rice lower the heat, cover and gently simmer for 15 minutes.

Remove the cinnamon sticks and add the remaining 2 tablespoons of butter and fluff the rice with a fork. Cook the racks of lamb for 10 minutes on the barbecue or grill for 20 minutes in a hot oven. Remove from the heat for 5 minutes. Carve and fan out over the rice.

Drizzle the dressing over the meat.

SERVES 6.

sage-grilled chicken souvlakia and olives

2 skinless, boneless chicken breast halves, cut into 16 or 24 pieces

½ cup fresh sage leaves

juice of ½ lemon

½ tablespoon strong-flavoured honey (I use Manuka Honey)

1 teaspoon mild wholegrain mustard

sea salt and freshly ground black pepper to taste

½ teaspoon ground bay leaf

9 tablespoons extra virgin olive oil

16 kalamata olives, pitted

16 small wooden skewers, soaked in water for 30 minutes, then drained

2 cups coarse fresh wholewheat breadcrumbs, lightly toasted

4 shallots, finely chopped

½ cup pine nuts, lightly toasted

¼ cup snipped fresh chives

sage sprigs and lemon wedges for garnish

In a medium bowl, combine the chicken and six of the sage leaves. Sprinkle with half the lemon juice. Combine the honey, mustard, pepper, bay leaf, remaining lemon juice and 2 tablespoons of the olive oil. Pour over the chicken and stir to coat each piece. Cover and set aside for 1 hour. Flatten each olive with the side of a heavy knife and put in a bowl. Stir in 1 tablespoon of the olive oil and set aside for 1 hour.

Prepare a charcoal grill. Prepare the breadcrumbs: stack the sage leaves and cut into thin ribbons. In a heavy frying pan over low heat, heat 2 tablespoons of the olive oil and cook the shallots for about 4 minutes or until soft. Add another 2 tablespoons of the oil, the pine nuts, the breadcrumbs, and the sage ribbons. Sauté, stirring occasionally, for about 4 minutes or until the breadcrumbs are golden and the sage is fragrant. Stir in the chives and season with salt and pepper; set aside and keep warm.

Thread 2–3 chicken pieces on each of 8 skewers and brush with the remaining 2 tablespoons of olive oil and any remaining marinade; discard the sage leaves. Thread 2 olives lengthwise onto each of the remaining 8 skewers. Brush the grill or a grill basket with olive oil and grill the chicken for 2 minutes. Place the olives on the grill or in the grill basket. Grill, turning both chicken and olives once, for 4–5 minutes, or until the chicken is golden brown and the olives are crinkled. Sprinkle the chicken with salt to taste and remove from the grill.

Spread the bread mixture over a warmed platter and arrange the souvlakia on top. Garnish with sage sprigs and lemon wedges. Serve immediately.

MAKES 8 MEZE OR 4 LIGHT MAIN-COURSE SERVINGS.

roast lamb with mustard stuffing

2 kg leg of lamb, tunnel-boned
6 potatoes, peeled and
    quartered
olive oil
fresh rosemary
sea salt

STUFFING
2 tablespoons Dijon mustard
1 cup fresh breadcrumbs
2 tablespoons honey
2 tablespoons chopped mint

Preheat the oven to 190ºC. Trim the lamb of any excess fat. To make the stuffing, combine the mustard, breadcrumbs, honey and mint. Place the stuffing in the lamb and tie with string to secure. Place the potatoes in a baking dish, drizzle with olive oil and sprinkle with rosemary and salt. Place a rack over the potatoes and place the lamb on top. Bake for 50–60 minutes or until the lamb and potatoes are tender. Serve with steamed green vegetables.

SERVES 4.

Chef's note: Ask your butcher to tunnel-bone the lamb.

honey glaze for pork

This works well on loin leg or whole suckling pig.

½ cup strong honey
2 tablespoons finely grated
    root ginger
3 cloves garlic, minced, with
    ¼ teaspoon salt
2 tablespoons soy sauce
½ cup pineapple juice
2–3 red chillies, seeded and
    finely chopped
1 tablespoon olive oil

Warm all together to blend. Cut deep cross-cut slashes in the pork rind and pour over the marinade. Marinate preferably overnight. Lift out of marinade and roast at 200ºC or barbecue, brushing on additional glaze as you near the end of the cooking time.

Chef's note: A little of the marinade brushed over pineapple or kumara and roasted is a great accompaniment.

cardamom and honey-glazed chicken with pumpkin couscous

MARINADE
4 tablespoons runny honey
2 tablespoons sherry
1 teaspoon cardamom seeds, ground
1 teaspoon peppercorns, ground

CHICKEN
6 chicken breasts
olive oil
12 slices lemon
Maldon sea salt and freshly ground black pepper

PUMPKIN COUSCOUS
350 g butternut, peeled and cut into 1 cm cubes
$\frac{1}{2}$ cup currants
Maldon sea salt and freshly ground black pepper
1 $\frac{1}{2}$ cups instant couscous prepared with 1 $\frac{1}{2}$ cups hot chicken stock or water
knob of butter
$\frac{1}{2}$ teaspoon cinnamon
3 tablespoons chopped mint

Recipe courtesy of Peta Mathias from *Sunday Star Times*, 29 July 2001.

Preheat oven to 200ºC. Prepare the marinade by warming the honey and sherry gently, then stir in the other ingredients. Allow to cool then add the chicken breasts for 5–10 minutes. In a frying pan heat a little olive oil over a medium-high heat and sear the chicken, skin-side down, until golden. Remove the chicken from the pan, leaving the pan on the heat but reducing to low. Place the lemon slices in a shallow roasting pan and lay the chicken breasts on top. Brush with the marinade, season with salt and pepper and place in the oven. Roast until golden and just cooked through — approximately 15 minutes, depending on size. Remove from the oven and rest for 10 minutes before serving.

Pumpkin couscous
Add the butternut to the frying pan and sauté until tender, turning from time to time. When it is cooked, add the currants to warm through and season with salt and pepper. Lift out with a slotted spoon and set aside. Add the butter and cinnamon to the couscous, fluff with a fork and fold through the butternut, currants, mint and a few of the lemon slices, chopped up. Adjust the seasoning if needed.

To serve: Pile the couscous onto a platter and lay the chicken breasts on top.

SERVES 6.

brendon's macadamia-stuffed chicken

Brendon created this recipe the day a huge bag of wonderful organic macadamias arrived in the kitchen, and the office girls went into raptures when asked to sample.

50 g mild honey,
　Clover/Farmhouse mix
10 g Kelp Seasoning
　(see page 17)
4 chicken breasts, single

MOUSSE
50 g chopped fresh herbs (e.g.
　parsley, tarragon or basil)
10 g honey
1 egg white
70 ml cream
60 g macadamia nuts, chopped
　and toasted
pinch nutmeg
salt and freshly ground black
　pepper

1 l chicken stock
bouquet garni (optional)

Remove the fillets from the chicken breasts.

Mousse
Process the chicken fillets in a food processor with the herbs, honey and egg white to a fine paste. In a bowl, fold the cream, chopped nuts, nutmeg, salt and pepper. This mixture should be very light. Place in the refrigerator.

Rub honey and kelp over the chicken. Spread a piece of microwave plastic wrap out to approximately 300 mm square, and place one breast skin-side down in the middle. Using a sharp knife, cut a pocket from where the fillet was removed from left to right. Spoon mousse into the pocket of the chicken, then roll the plastic wrap around the chicken and tie both ends tightly, making sure all the air is removed from the parcel. Wrap the parcel in tin foil, twisting both ends. Repeat this method for the remaining chicken breasts.

The parcels can be kept like this overnight, which helps the honey flavour the chicken.

In a large poaching pan, bring the chicken stock to a simmer. Add the chicken parcels, making sure they are covered with stock. Place a tightly fitting lid on the poaching pan and simmer for 15–20 minutes or until the parcels are firm to touch.

Remove and place on a rack to rest, remove the foil and plastic wrap, cut and serve. The liquid from the parcel can be drizzled over the chicken as a light jus. This meal can also be served cold.

SERVES 4.

salmon with honey mustard dressing

This recipe is from The Best of Ruth Pretty *and I vote this as one of the best honey mustard dressings around.*

**4 x 150 g pieces of fresh salmon
(bone out and skin on)
1 recipe Salmon Marinade
olive oil for brushing
1 recipe Honey Mustard Dressing**

**SALMON MARINADE
½ cup olive oil
1 tablespoon soy sauce
1 garlic clove, finely chopped**

**1 clove garlic, finely chopped
1 tablespoon finely chopped
red onion
½ teaspoon mustard powder
2 tablespoons liquid honey
1 teaspoon lemon zest
4 tablespoons lemon juice
4 tablespoons olive oil
Maldon sea salt and freshly
ground black pepper
2 tablespoons currants
2 medium tomatoes, blanched,
peeled, seeded and chopped
2 tablespoons finely chopped
Italian parsley**

To make marinade, combine the oil, soy sauce and garlic in a small bowl.

Place the salmon in a non-reactive dish with the marinade and leave for a minimum of 20 minutes or up to 1 hour. Preheat oven to 220ºC. Spray or brush a low-sided baking tray with olive oil. Remove the salmon from the marinade and place skin-side down on the tray. Bake in the oven for 6–8 minutes or until the salmon is cooked medium rare. Serve with Honey Mustard Dressing and asparagus.

Honey mustard dressing

I first enjoyed this dressing with salmon prepared by Michael Lee-Richards as part of a perfect Pinot Pairing session.

Combine the first eight ingredients in a bowl and whisk to blend. Add the currants and set aside to allow them to plump up. Before serving, stir in the tomatoes and parsley.

SERVES 4.

Chef's note: Salmon stays very moist when you cook it with the skin on.

watermelon, feta prawn salad with rose honey vinaigrette

This combination of great summer flavours is a feast for both the eyes and tastebuds.

1 watermelon
200 g rose prawns
150 g feta cheese
8 purple basil leaves
2 rose geranium leaves

Slice the watermelon in half, lie on a flat surface and slice down. Cut the rind away, seed and cube. Mix with prawns and cover with feta cheese.

ROSE HONEY VINAIGRETTE
2 tablespoons olive oil
1 teaspoon Rose Honey
2 tablespoons White Wine Honeygar
salt and freshly ground pink peppercorns

Combine all the ingredients and pour over the salad.

Garnish with purple basil tips and rose geranium leaves that have been very finely chopped.

honeyed fish fillets

1 teaspoon freshly grated ginger
3 tablespoons Bush Honey
1 tablespoon fresh orange juice
1 tablespoon orange rind
3 shallots, thinly sliced
1 teaspoon soy sauce (or teriyaki sauce)
freshly ground black pepper
$\frac{1}{4}$ teaspoon chilli powder
500 g fish fillets

Combine all the ingredients, except the fish, in a saucepan. Heat gently to melt the honey. Place the fish in a dish and pour over the marinade. Refrigerate for 1–2 hours. Place the fish fillets on a lightly oiled barbecue or in a non-stick frying pan. Cook on medium heat for approximately 3 minutes each side. During the cooking, baste generously with the marinade. To serve, pour any remaining reduced marinade over fish.

SERVES 2.

baked fish with lemon glaze

500 g fresh skinned and boneless fish fillets, or whole cleaned, scaled fish

1 teaspoon finely chopped fresh red chilli

1 garlic clove, finely chopped

$\frac{1}{2}$ teaspoon salt

2 teaspoons strong honey

2–3 tablespoons sharp lemon or lime juice

zest of 1 large lemon (a sharp variety like Lisbon)

freshly ground black pepper

$\frac{1}{4}$ cup freshly chopped coriander

Preheat the oven to 220ºC. Arrange the fish fillets in a baking dish. Finely chop the chilli and garlic in $\frac{1}{2}$ teaspoon salt. Combine with the honey (warm if necessary to soften), lemon juice and zest. Mix well and spread over the fish. Season with pepper. Roast for 6–8 minutes until fish is just opaque and cooked. Sprinkle with fresh coriander.

Chef's note: Some finely diced fresh capsicum could be tossed in the glaze then layered on the fish before baking.

Baked Fish with Lemon Glaze served with Honey Mustard Dressing (see page 64)

summer fish

2 tablespoons olive oil

1 red capsicum, cored, seeded
    and cut into strips

1 yellow capsicum, cored,
    seeded and cut into strips

1 red onion, halved and sliced

6 stalks broccolini

1 courgette, sliced

$\frac{1}{2}$ fresh corn cob, sliced and
    precooked

2 fresh fish fillets, skinned and
    boned (I use gurnard)

2 tablespoons flour

salt and freshly ground
    black pepper

2 cloves garlic, finely chopped

2 tablespoons honey

zest and juice 1 large lemon

bunch of fresh mint,
    roughly chopped

Heat 1 tablespoon of olive oil in a pan. Add the capsicums, onion, broccolini, courgette and corn and sauté for about 5 minutes until cooked, colourful but still firm to touch. Remove to a warm serving dish. Put the remaining olive oil in the pan and heat. Toss the fish in flour seasoned with salt and pepper, and pan-fry till just cooked through. When you turn over the fish, add the chopped garlic. As soon as the fish is cooked, remove and place on the vegetables. Warm the honey, mix with the lemon juice and zest and swirl around the pan. Pour over the fish then sprinkle with fresh mint.

It's best eaten immediately, but can be eaten cooled.

Chef's note: Baby new potatoes are nice served on the side.

grilled fish fillets served with mango, ginger and honeygar dressing

This low-fat yet full-flavoured dressing is also great on chicken or with steamed vegetables.

1 mango
1 tablespoon grated root ginger
1 fresh red chilli, seeded and
   finely chopped
2–3 tablespoons BeesOnline
   White Wine and Clover
   Honeygar
2 tablespoons lemon or
   lime juice
2 tablespoons chopped
   fresh coriander
whole snapper or fillets
bunch of young spinach leaves
   (either raw for salad or can
   be very lightly steamed)
few cherry tomatoes or slivered
   red capsicum for garnish

Slice the mango in half. Peel and slice one half for garnish, and put the remaining flesh into the food processor or blender. Add the ginger, chilli, honeygar, lemon or lime juice and fresh coriander. Process until smooth. For a more liquid consistency adjust with a little water and blend again. Reserve sauce.

If using whole snapper slash the sides and rub with a little oil. Put the fish under the grill or on the barbecue for 5–6 minutes, turning if necessary. Place on the spinach, tomatoes or slivered capsicum and reserved mango slices. Serve with sauce and rice or crispy French bread.

SERVES 2–4.

seared baby calamari salad with Thai honey dressing

DRESSING

1 clove garlic
2 teaspoons lemon grass
1 tablespoon fresh coriander
1 tablespoon fresh basil
2 chillies (1 red, 1 green),
   seeded and finely sliced
2 teaspoons finely grated
   fresh ginger
zest of $\frac{1}{2}$ lime
salt and freshly ground black
   pepper to taste
2 teaspoons Chilli Honey
   (see page 17)
juice of 2 limes
juice of 1 orange
50 ml hazelnut oil (or lemon-
   infused avocado oil)

500 g baby squid tubes
1 small bunch baby bok choy
2 handfuls mesclun
$\frac{1}{2}$ red onion, finely sliced
1 orange, segmented

To make the dressing, finely chop the first five ingredients. Whisk them together with the remaining ingredients. Marinate the squid in the dressing for 30 minutes.

Heat a ridged pan and sear the squid (1–2 minutes). Turn, remove, then add the dressing to deglaze the pan. Toss in the bok choy and cook until it wilts. Place on a serving dish with the mesclun, red onion and orange segments. Top with the squid and drizzle a little dressing over the top.

SERVES 2.

honeyed trout

Also nice with other fish if you have not got time to whip off and catch a trout.

55 g butter (plus extra for greasing)
3 onions, thinly sliced
2 teaspoons ground cumin
salt and freshly ground black pepper
2 tablespoons BeesOnline full-flavoured Bush Blend Honey
150 ml water
150 ml dry white wine
1 large or 2 smaller trout, gutted and cleaned
115 g buttered mushrooms, thinly sliced

Preheat the oven to 160ºC and generously grease an ovenproof dish with butter.

Melt the butter in a saucepan over medium heat and soften the onions in it. Stir in the cumin and season with salt and pepper. Add the honey, water and the wine and gently simmer for 2–3 minutes.

Arrange the cooked onions in a layer on the bottom of the prepared oven dish, place the fish on top and scatter over the mushrooms, tucking a few inside, and dot with butter. Cover and bake for about 25 minutes or until cooked.

Using a slotted spoon, transfer the fish and vegetables to a warmed serving dish, pour the juices over and serve immediately.

SERVES 6.

fillet of john dory with pine nuts, onions and sultanas

This recipe is courtesy of Catherine Bell of Epicurean. We suggest you try replacing the white wine vinegar with BeesOnline White Wine Honeygar. You could use BeesOnline Matua Estate, Bush Blend or Farmhouse Honey in this recipe.

650 g fillet of John Dory cut into 2.5 cm strips
flour
½–¾ cup extra virgin olive oil
freshly ground black pepper to taste
2 medium onions, cut into slivers
6 tablespoons sultanas, soaked in hot water for 10 minutes and drained
¾ cup pine nuts, toasted
1 ½ cups dry white wine
100 ml white wine vinegar
5–6 tablespoons honey

Dredge the pieces of fish in flour. Heat 4–5 tablespoons of oil in a large heavy frying pan over a medium-high heat. Sauté the fish quickly in batches until golden brown, adding more oil as needed. Transfer to a large shallow serving dish and sprinkle with pepper.

Heat an additional 3 tablespoons of oil in the same pan and sauté the onions for 8–10 minutes until golden but not browned. Scatter the onion over the fish along with the sultanas and pine nuts.

To make the dressing, combine the wine, vinegar and honey. Pour over the fish. Cool to room temperature. Cover and refrigerate for 3–4 hours or overnight. Return to room temperature before serving.

SERVES 6.

desserts

rustic fruit tart with tawari honey sabayon

I love using Tawari Honey for scrummy desserts because of its rich, buttery, almost chocolate flavour.

1 phyllo pastry sheet
melted butter
fresh fruit in season (apples, quince, figs, pears, peaches, nectarines, etc.)
25 g butter per serve
Tawari Honey — 1 dessertspoon per serve
lemon juice to taste

TAWARI HONEY SABAYON

1 egg yolk
1 whole egg
1 capful dark rum
1 dessertspoon warm Tawari Honey

Preheat the oven to 180ºC. At the Café we prefer making individual tarts, using seven 12 cm diameter flan tins. Cut the sheet of phyllo into four squares (best to use kitchen scissors) just larger than your flan tin. Lightly brush butter on the bottom of the tin. Brush one square of phyllo with butter and place in the tin. Repeat until all the squares are used. Press gently into the base of the flan tin. Blind bake until just golden and crisp. Cool. When ready to serve, peel and slice fresh fruit. Melt the butter in a pan and toss the fruit. Add the honey and a squeeze of lemon to taste and sauté gently until the fruit is tender.

Meanwhile make the sabayon. Whisk the ingredients at high speed in a bowl standing in hot water until the mixture is thick and fluffy. A double boiler is perfect for this. Assemble the tart by piling the warm fruit into the phyllo pastry shell and spoon some of the sabayon over the top. Serve immediately.

SERVES 1.

Chef's note: You can also make larger tarts using the same method, but increasing the sabayon accordingly.

pink peppercorn pavlova

At BeesOnline we love stepping our tastebuds outside the square. I came across this spiced-up meringue variation in Hong Kong. Here's BeesOnline's version.

MERINGUE
4 egg whites
pinch salt
250 g castor sugar
1 teaspoon vanilla extract
1 teaspoon White Wine Honeygar
1 teaspoon cornflour
2 teaspoons pink peppercorns, crushed

300 ml cream
1–2 tablespoons honey
fresh berries to decorate

Preheat the oven to 200ºC. Using an electric beater, beat the egg whites and a pinch of salt until soft peaks form. Add 3–4 tablespoons of the castor sugar and beat again until all sugar has dissolved. Add half the remaining sugar, beat again until smooth and repeat until all sugar is incorporated and the mixture is glossy and smooth. Add the vanilla and Honeygar, then the cornflour and lastly the crushed peppercorns.
Spread onto a non-stick baking paper-lined oven tray. Place in the oven and reduce the heat immediately to 120ºC. After 1 hour turn the oven off and leave to cool in the oven. Overnight works well.

Whip the cream with a little honey to sweeten and add fresh berries. Pile on top of the meringue and sprinkle with icing sugar.

SERVES 4–6.

exotic Middle Eastern honey- creamed rice

Sweet rice puddings are comfort food all around the world, and honey increases the mouth feel. This one is a favourite with my family.

60 ml mild honey
1.5 l milk
150 g white short grain rice
1 teaspoon ground cardamom
35 g currants
1 tablespoon chopped toasted pistachio nuts
cream and extra honey to drizzle

Mix the honey and milk in a large heavy-bottomed saucepan. Stir until the honey has melted and bring to the boil. Add the rice, cardamom and currants. Stir, reduce the heat and, stirring frequently, simmer uncovered until the rice is creamy and soft. This takes about 40 minutes. Best served warm, topped with nuts. Drizzle with cream and extra warm honey.

SERVES 4.

Chef's note: If you plan to eat the rice cold add a little more milk to soften it as the rice will thicken on cooling.

orange and honey crème caramels

The Italians call crème caramels latté imperials. This is a great twist on a very classic theme.

260 g Farmhouse Honey
   (Citrus or Orchard Blends
   would complement well)
1 tablespoon water
4 eggs
550 ml milk
finely grated rind of ½ orange
pinch of cardamom
90 g roasted peeled hazelnuts
extra honey to drizzle

Preheat oven to 170ºC. Heat two-thirds of the honey with the water in a small heavy-bottomed saucepan until rich and golden. Stir as the honey comes to the boil, then reduce the heat to medium and watch carefully. As soon as the colour deepens, remove from the heat and allow the bubbles to subside, then divide the mixture between six 150 ml ramekins. Warm the remaining honey and whisk in the eggs until just combined. Then whisk in the milk, orange rind and cardamom. Pour the mixture over the honey caramel. Cook 'au bain marie' in a roasting dish waterbath with water coming halfway up the outside of the ramekin. Bake for 20–30 minutes until the custards are just set. Remove from the waterbath. Cool, then refrigerate for several hours before inverting on plates to serve. Top with hazelnuts drizzled with honey.

honeyed panna cotta

Honey seems to have been connected with love and sensuality since the beginning of time — even the holiday that newlyweds take is called a honeymoon.

250 ml cream
2 tablespoons castor sugar
2 tablespoons honey (try
  BeesOnline Farmhouse, Tawari
  or Pohutukawa)
1 vanilla pod, split
2 teaspoons powdered gelatine
90 ml milk

Heat the cream, sugar, honey and vanilla pod in a small saucepan, stirring to dissolve the sugar. Gently bring to the boil, then remove from the heat. Whisk in the gelatine until dissolved. Add the milk and mix well. Pour into moulds and refrigerate for approximately 1 hour before serving. Dip each mould in warm water to release.

Chef's note: When turning out a gelatine-based dish, wet the serving plate first, to allow you to position the food, then wipe around with a dry cloth to fix it in place.

baked honey and citrus ricotta cheesecakes

1 measure shortcrust pastry
(your favourite recipe or try
our Honey Shortcrust
Pastry below)
250 g ricotta cheese
2 tablespoons cream
3 tablespoons mild honey (try
BeesOnline Farmhouse or
Woodhill Clover)
½ teaspoon vanilla extract
2 eggs
finely grated rind of 1 lemon
15 g BeesOnline Honeyed
Orange Peel

Roll out the pastry and line 4.5 cm miniature tartlet tins, or use larger if you prefer. Preheat the oven to 200ºC. Combine all remaining ingredients, except the peel, in a food processor or with a handheld blender. Mix until smooth. Spoon the mixture into the pastry bases, filling about three-quarters full and place a small strip of honeyed peel on top. Bake in a preheated oven at 200ºC for 15–20 minutes or until the pastry is golden and the filling has risen and set.

MAKES 1 LARGE OR 24 MINI CHEESECAKES.

120 g butter
2 tablespoons mild honey
(BeesOnline Farmhouse or
Woodhill Clover)
½ cup milk (or ⅓ cup milk and
1 egg yolk)
2 cups self-raising flour

Honey shortcrust pastry
Cream the butter and honey. Beat in the milk (and egg yolk if used). Gradually add the flour, and stir to form a dry dough ball. Roll out to a thickness of 5–6 mm, and use as required. Chill before baking to avoid shrinkage.

whisky oranges with honeyed cream

Here's a BeesOnline variation of a classic winter dessert.

4 large or 8 small oranges
$\frac{1}{2}$ **cup water**
$\frac{1}{2}$ **cup mild honey**
$\frac{1}{2}$ **cup Scotch whisky**

Using a serrated knife, finely peel the oranges carefully over a bowl, removing all the pith and being careful to retain the nice shape. Slice and arrange in a bowl. For an interesting presentation slice the oranges, toothpick them back together then stack in a glass bowl. Bring the water and honey to the boil and simmer for 2 minutes. Remove from the heat, then add the whisky and allow to cool. Pour over the oranges and chill. Serve with Honeyed Cream.

Chef's note: You may wish to vary the basic recipe by adding whole cloves, cinnamon sticks, whole allspice berries, or star anise to Honey and Whisky Syrup. I have also included some thin strips of zest.

1 cup cream
2 tablespoons Scotch whisky
1 tablespoon honey

Honeyed cream
Gently whip the cream and as it is thickening add the whisky and honey and continue beating until thick but still soft.

SERVES 4.

honey tarte tatin

1 tablespoon butter
½ cup BeesOnline
   Farmhouse Honey
4 tart apples (Granny Smith
   is best)
¼ teaspoon ground cinnamon
sweet short pastry for
   200 mm pie
lightly whipped cream and
   Farmhouse Honey to serve

Generously butter the bottom and sides of a 200 mm ovenproof pan — preferably cast iron. Pour the honey into the pan and warm. Peel, core and slice the apples and place curved-side down in the pan, arranged in curving pattern. Sprinkle with cinnamon. Roll out the pastry and place on top, tucking the edges between the apples and the sides of the pan. Bake at 200ºC until risen and golden (approximately 30 minutes). Let cool in the pan for 5 minutes before inverting onto a serving platter and serving with lightly whipped cream sweetened with warm Farmhouse Honey.

SERVES 4.

honey syllabub

The recipe comes courtesy of Gates Honey Bureau.

500 ml cream
5 tablespoons runny honey
150 ml white wine
2 tablespoons lemon juice

Whisk all ingredients together until stiff enough to spoon into glasses. Almost fill the glasses and then chill. Serve with wafer-type biscuits or shortbread fingers.

SERVES 4.

Champagne and honey sorbet

This recipe comes courtesy of Moët & Chandon (London) Ltd. Try it after a romantic dinner.

½ **cup sugar**
400 ml water
¾ **of a 750 ml bottle Champagne**
juice of 1 lemon
1 egg white, stiffly beaten
¼ **cup castor sugar**
**1 tablespoon honey (try
    Farmhouse or maybe Tawari)**

Make the syrup by warming the sugar and water, stirring until all the sugar has dissolved. Bring to the boil, then remove from the heat and cool.

Half freeze the syrup, Champagne and lemon juice in an ice-cream maker. Make a meringue by whisking the egg white until shiny, adding half the castor sugar and whisking again for approximately 1 minute, then adding the remaining sugar and the honey and whisking until the mixture is stiff, smooth and shiny. Fold into the half-frozen Champagne mix. Freeze until required. Serve in frozen sorbet glasses.

SERVES 4–6.

pohutukawa honey and cardamom ice cream

An exotic blend that is scrumptious with roasted stone fruits.

300 ml milk
300 ml cream
7 cardamom pods, crushed (or 1/2 teaspoon freshly ground cardamom)
1/2 cup Pohutukawa or BeesOnline Coastal Blend Honey
4 egg yolks

Carefully bring the milk, cream and crushed cardamom pods just to the boil. Then immediately remove the saucepan from the heat. Heat the honey until nearly boiling (this can be done in a microwave for about 30 seconds). Whisk the egg yolks, then pour the hot honey over in a steady stream, beating all the time. Whisk in the warm milk mixture. Wash the saucepan and then strain the egg yolk and milk mixture back into the saucepan.

Stir the mixture slowly over a low heat with a wooden spoon until the custard just coats the back of the spoon. Do not let the mixture boil, otherwise you risk curdling. Check the seasoning, remembering that the flavour will soften when frozen so you may wish to enhance it with a little vanilla, some molten white chocolate or Baileys liqueur.

Transfer to a bowl, cool to room temperature, then cover and chill in the fridge. When chilled, place in an ice-cream machine and process according to the manufacturer's instructions. If you do not have an ice-cream maker, freeze in a shallow container and whisk every 30 minutes to break up the large ice crystals.

MAKES APPROXIMATELY 1 LITRE.

honey ice cream

A decadent summer treat that is scrumptious with freshly roasted peaches or apricots. Use your favourite honey — mine would be Pohutukawa or Tawari, but this recipe would be equally as nice with Clover or Manuka.

4 eggs
¼ cup honey
2 cups cream

Beat the eggs until thick and creamy. Bring the honey nearly to the boil, then pour over the eggs and whisk until mixed. Pour the mixture back into the saucepan and cook over a low heat, stirring constantly, until the mixture thickens a little. Do not let the mixture boil. Pour the mixture into a bowl and set aside to cool thoroughly. When cool, add the cream and chill in the refrigerator. Freeze in an ice-cream machine as instructed by the manufacturer and store in a covered container in the freezer until ready to use.

Chef's note: Great served with Honey Tuiles.

Honey tuiles

These light-as-air crisp wafers are a wonderful accompaniment to freshly made ice-cream syllabubs or sorbets.

50 g liquid honey (Clover)
50 g castor sugar
2 egg whites
50 g white flour
50 g unsalted butter
2 teaspoons sesame seeds

Melt the honey and sugar together. Add the egg whites and flour and mix well. Melt the butter, then stir in with the sesame seeds. Cool before spreading thinly in the shape of a circle onto greased, floured baking sheets or silicon mats. Bake until golden, remove from the oven, cool, then remove from the sheet and fold over a wooden spoon handle to create taco-shell shapes.

walnut pikelets

Fresh pikelets are a very New Zealand home-style treat. This version, dripping with warm honey and honeyed cream, is always a huge hit. I make these in the food processor or blender for added speed.

⅓ cup ground walnuts
½ cup milk
1 ½ tablespoons butter, melted
¾ cup standard white flour
1 heaped teaspoon baking powder
1 heaped tablespoon Farmhouse Honey
1 large egg

Grind the walnuts first, then add all the other ingredients. Blend until smooth and bubbly. Cook in small spoonfuls on a lightly greased heavy pan or griddle. Best served warm with honey and cream.

Chef's note: For another fabulous pikelet variation try substituting long thread coconut instead of walnuts. When doing this I use 1 cup standard flour, whiz the mixture, then stir in 2–3 tablespoons long thread coconut before cooking. Serve these with Honeyed Ginger (see page 17) and cream.

honey scones

The BeesOnline Café has become famous for its scones. Staff and customers alike hang out around the kitchen door for the chef's daily offering. So we list here a random selection to inspire you. The base recipe was my grandmother's; she used cream, so for special scones I do the same and add a beaten egg, which increases their lifespan so they have that fresh-from-the-oven taste all day.

3 cups flour
4 ½ teaspoons baking powder
¼ teaspoon salt
75 g butter
2 tablespoons warmed honey (or a chunk, approximately 2 tablespoons, fork-broken honeycomb)
1–1 ½ cups creamy milk (half milk, half cream if you can)
1 egg, beaten

Preheat the oven to 230ºC. Sift the dry ingredients and rub in the butter. Make a well in the centre of the flour mixture. Add the honey. Blend the creamy milk and egg (reserving a little of the mixture for glazing). Pour the milk and egg mixture into the well on top of the honey, then, using a knife, mix the liquid ingredients into the dry ingredients lightly and quickly until a soft dough is formed. Turn onto a floured board and roll or pat lightly into shape (approximately 2.5–3 cm thick). Cut out the scones and place on an oven tray. Glaze with a small amount of the leftover creamy milky egg mixture; brush on tops only using a pastry brush. Sprinkle on a topping if desired. Bake in a hot oven (230ºC) for 8–10 minutes until risen and golden.

Chef's note: Whatever fresh fruit is on hand goes to flavour our scones. We serve them with a choice of two honeys and Honeyed Cream (see page 82). Here are a few of our latest creations:

Pumpkin and Date	Orange and Pear
White Chocolate and Banana	Blackberry and Apple
Feijoa, Lemonade and Pear	Spiced Chai and Ginger
Apple and Honeyed Ginger	Peach and Vanilla
Plum and Feijoa	Honey and Macadamia
Plum and Orange	Grapefruit and Pear

rose honey cakes

These lovely little cakes are perfect for a Mother's Day or a girls' afternoon tea. Alternatively, perhaps a romantic dessert ...

1 ¼ cups canola oil

2 cups rose sugar
(see recipe below)

3 eggs

¼ cup Clover or Thistle Honey, warmed

grated rind of 1 lemon

¼ cup lemon juice — Lisbon for preference, which has a sharp lemon flavour

¾ cup natural yoghurt (I use the thick Greek sort)

3 cups self-raising flour

4 rose geranium leaves, finely chopped

BeesOnline Manuka Honey Syrup (optional)

Preheat the oven to 160ºC. Whisk the oil and sugar with an electric beater to combine — approximately 1–2 minutes. Then add the eggs one at a time, beating until thick and creamy. Add the warm honey, lemon rind, juice and yoghurt. Blend again. Sift in the self-raising flour and beat until just mixed. Fold in rose geranium leaves.

Pour into individual ⅓ cup-capacity half-round cake moulds or large muffin tins, and cook for approximately 10 minutes until risen and firm to a gentle touch. Cool slightly before turning out. Pour BeesOnline Manuka Honey Syrup over while still warm. Alternatively, drizzle over rose-tinted glacé icing and decorate with crystallised rose petals.

Rose sugar
Store 4 cups of castor sugar with a handful of rose geranium leaves for at least 7 days to infuse flavour. Dried leaves can stay in the sugar indefinitely, or can be sieved out if you prefer.

Chef's notes: For an exotic Middle Eastern touch add 2 tablespoons of whole aniseeds to the mixture before baking.

Rose petals can be crystallised by brushing both sides of the fresh dry rose petals with egg white that has been gently broken up with a fork. Then drench in castor sugar. Store in a warm dry place. When harvesting rose petals ensure that they have not been subjected to sprays.

If you do not have access to rose geranium leaves, you could substitute 8 highly perfumed spray-free rose petals.

low-fat pear and ginger muffins

This recipe uses comb honey which, when baked, produces a moist muffin without the use of fat. The wax emulsifies in the batter. Humans don't digest beeswax, so it's an inert lipid in our systems but it makes for an interesting and healthy alternative on the ever-popular muffin theme. Best served warm.

200 g comb honey
2 large eggs
1 ½ cups self-raising flour
1 ½ pears, peeled and diced
**2 tablespoons diced
    preserved ginger**
icing sugar to dust

Preheat the oven to 180ºC. Place the comb honey and eggs in a bowl and roughly mash with a fork. Combine lightly with the flour, then fold in the pears and half the ginger.

Place in well-greased non-stick muffin tins. Top with remaining diced ginger pieces and bake for approximately 20 minutes until just cooked through and lightly golden. Dust with icing sugar.

MAKES 12.

honey and almond lace biscuits

These are delicious on their own or look pretty balanced on the side of a fruity or creamy dessert.

125 g butter
½ cup sugar
**110 ml BeesOnline
    Farmhouse Honey**
⅔ cup flour
½ teaspoon baking soda
½ teaspoon cream of tartar
35 g flaked almonds

Preheat the oven to 180ºC. Place the butter, sugar and honey in a saucepan and sit over a gentle heat until melted. Remove from the heat and add the flour, baking soda and cream of tartar. Stir with a wooden spoon until smooth, then add the almonds.

Bake in three lots of four. Cook in dessertspoonful lots on baking paper for about 7 minutes until bubbly all over. Watch carefully so they do not burn. Cool for a couple of minutes on the baking tray. When the biscuits can hold their shape when gently lifted with a palette knife, either twist into rosette shapes, drape over a rolling pin or roll like brandy snaps. Cool well before storing in an airtight container.

MAKES 12.

honey and fig cakes

My friend Liz Curtis makes this fabulous moist honey and fig cake. At the Café we use the recipe to make little upright individual cakes. With a sliver of honeycomb on the top, they are probably our most popular cakes.

½ **cup castor sugar**
125 g butter
¼ **cup runny Clover Honey**
2 eggs
½ **cup milk**
250 g dried figs, finely chopped
1 ¾ **cups self-raising flour, sifted**
½ **cup Farmhouse or**
  Clover Honey

Preheat the oven to 160ºC and grease 12 individual cake or muffin tins or one 20 cm springform tin. Process the sugar, butter and honey in a kitchen whiz until creamy. Add eggs, milk and half of the dried figs and blend together. Pour this mixture into a bowl and mix in the flour and the remaining figs. Divide between the prepared tins and bake for 15–20 minutes or until a skewer comes out clean. Cool. Warm half a cup of honey and brush over the cakes.

Chef's note: If figs are unavailable this is equally as good with prunes or apricots. For a special occasion presoak the dried fruit in liqueur.

MAKES 12 INDIVIDUAL CAKES OR 1 LARGE CAKE.

lavender and honey mead biscuits

This special recipe is a variation on an old French pastry. Because I'm a country person my rambling garden is important to me. I enjoy wandering and picking handfuls of flowers and herbs. Herbs in the flower arrangements and flowers in the cooking make for inspirational meals.

130 g plain flour
pinch salt
85 g Lavender Sugar (see below)
55 g butter
2–2 ½ tablespoons honey mead (First Knight liqueur is excellent) or use a sweet dessert wine
20 leaves fresh lavender, finely chopped, or 10 lavender heads

Preheat the oven to 190ºC. Sift the flour and salt and mix with all but 1 tablespoon of the Lavender Sugar. Rub in the butter until the mixture resembles breadcrumbs, then add the honey mead and lavender leaves (or lavender heads) and stir gently until the mixture binds together. Roll out the mixture on a floured board to form a rectangle 3 mm thick. With a sharp knife, cut out 8 cm x 3 cm strips of the biscuit dough. Give each strip one twist to form a bow and place on a greased baking tray. Bake at 190ºC for 6–10 minutes until the edges just turn brown. Sprinkle with the remaining Lavender Sugar. Cool on oven trays.

MAKES 12.

6 fresh French lavender heads, roughly chopped
2 cups castor sugar

Lavender sugar
Mix the lavender and sugar and store in an airtight container for 1–2 weeks, shaking occasionally. Sift through a fine sieve.

Christmas honey nut tarts

These wonderfully scrumptious little buttery tarts are an excellent alternative to Christmas mince pies at your festive soirées.

60 g butter, melted and cooled
2 eggs
juice of $\frac{1}{2}$ lemon
$\frac{1}{2}$ cup soft brown sugar
1 x 250 g jar BeesOnline Roasted Honey Nuts (see page 17)

PASTRY
125 g butter
1 cup high-grade flour
$\frac{1}{2}$ cup icing sugar

Preheat the oven to 160ºC.

To make the pastry, put all the ingredients in a blender. Whiz to a fine blend. A little chilled water (and egg yolk if a rich dough is required) may be added in 'pulses' by the food processor until a ball is forming. Gently knead into a ball. Break off little pieces and roll into balls approximately 30 mm in diameter. Finger-press into lightly greased mini tartlet tins then chill.

Make the filling by blending the butter, eggs, lemon and brown sugar, then mix in the Roasted Honey Nuts. Spoon into the pastry shells and bake for 10–15 minutes or until golden brown. Leave in the tins for a few moments until firm enough to gently lift out and cool.

MAKES 24.

Try serving this with Honeyed Cream (see page 82).

semolina, coconut and honey cake

2 cups finely ground semolina
1 cup desiccated coconut
½ cup castor sugar
200 g butter, melted
1 cup milk

HONEY SYRUP
1 cup mild honey
⅓ cup water
2 tablespoons lemon juice

Preheat the oven to 175ºC. Combine the semolina, coconut and castor sugar in a bowl. Mix the melted butter and milk and pour into the dry ingredients. Mix thoroughly, then pour into a greased dish 20 cm x 20 cm x 1.5 cm and bake for 30 minutes. Do not use a loose-bottomed tin for this recipe. While still hot, cut into rectangles or diamonds as they do in the Middle East. Pour over the hot Honey Syrup, then allow to cool. Serve at room temperature.

To make the syrup, dissolve the honey in the water. Bring nearly to the boil, add the lemon juice then pour over the hot cake.

Chef's note: For syrup variations, substitute 1–2 tablespoons of water for Grand Marnier liqueur and add 1 tablespoon of orange blossom water or use Rose Honey (see page 17) for the syrup and add the zest of 1 orange. BeesOnline Manuka Honey Syrup could also be poured straight over the top of this cake.

paraoa reka

As a child I remember afternoon treats at a friend's house of deep-fried 'Maori Bread' with jam and cream. Looking for typical 'Kiwi' cuisine for our Café, I rang Rota for his mum's recipe. At the Café we make it into little balls, like the loukoumathes (Greek doughnuts) they serve on the streets of Athens in newspaper cones, and then we bathe them in puddles of Manuka Honey Syrup.

3 cups self-raising flour
1 cup warm water
1 cup milk
100 g butter, melted
1 heaped teaspoon baking powder
mild vegetable oil for deep frying (such as canola or grapeseed)

Mix all the ingredients together well and fry in little balls in oil. Drain and serve with Honey Syrup.

Honey syrup
Our prepared Manuka Honey Syrup is excellent, but try making your own with:

½ cup Bush Honey
juice and zest of 1 lemon

and sprinkle with ground cinnamon.

honey syrups

Honey syrups are delicious over warm cakes, Greek yoghurts, rice or porridge or maybe fresh fruit.

250 ml honey
100 ml water, juice, wine or liqueur
flavouring to taste

Base recipe
Combine over heat, stirring until just under boiling. Remove from the heat. Skim or strain as necessary.

Great flavour suggestions:

All citrus fruit peel	Fresh mint	Concentrated apple syrups
Fruit juices	Lemongrass	
Fresh berries	Rose or lavender	Liqueurs or coffee instead of
Cinnamon sticks	Saffron	100 ml water
Star anise	Cloves	Herbal teas

chocolate honey and espresso sandwiches

At the BeesOnline Honey Centre and Café these often sit on the counter in a glass jar, tempting the coffee connoisseurs. Easy and funky nibbles.

200 g plain flour
$\frac{1}{2}$ cup cocoa powder
$\frac{1}{2}$ teaspoon salt
175 g butter
$\frac{3}{4}$ cup icing sugar
$\frac{1}{4}$ cup Clover Honey

ESPRESSO FILLING
60 g soft butter
500 g icing sugar, sifted
$\frac{1}{4}$ cup freshly brewed espresso
   coffee

Preheat the oven to 190ºC. Sift flour, cocoa and salt into a bowl. Cream the butter, icing sugar and honey until light and fluffy, then gradually add flour mixture and beat until well combined. Roll into small walnut-sized balls. Place on baking sheets, then press with a fork through the middle to squash. Bake at 190ºC for 8–10 minutes until firm to touch.

Cool on trays. Unfilled biscuits will keep for several days.

For the espresso filling, combine all ingredients in a heatproof bowl over a saucepan of simmering water and stir until smooth. Remove the bowl from the heat and refrigerate for 20 minutes, stirring every 5 minutes or until thick and creamy. Sandwich the biscuits together with a small amount of filling.

MAKES 24.

honey baklava

Once upon a lifetime ago I lived in Greece, mostly on Crete, to be precise. The sun, the food and the wine remain etched in my memory, such as honey and thick ewes' milk yoghurt for breakfast and thyme honey syrup drizzled over intricate little pastries. Baklava is probably the easiest dish to recreate.

1 ½ **cups walnuts, blanched almonds or pistachios, or a mix of all three**
2 **tablespoons sugar**
pinch salt
approximately 150 g butter, melted
1 **packet phyllo pastry**

Preheat the oven to 175ºC. Roughly chop the nuts and mix with the sugar and salt. Using a pastry brush lightly butter a Swiss roll tin. Open the phyllo and if warm cover with a clean tea towel so that it does not dry out and become brittle. Brush a sheet of phyllo pastry with butter, then sprinkle over 2 tablespoons of nuts. Repeat this process, ending with a buttered top. With a sharp knife score through the top pastry to make cutting lines. Traditionally these are done in diamonds, which I find frustratingly uneconomic, so I usually do squares which I then cut into triangles. Bake until crisp and lightly golden — about 30–40 minutes.

Meanwhile make the syrup.

Honey syrup

1 ¼ **cups strong Bush Honey**
juice and finely grated rind of 1 lemon
2 **cinnamon sticks**

Bring all to the boil, then cool.

While the baklava is still hot pour the cool syrup over and cut the triangles right through. Cool in the dish and serve later at room temperature.

Chef's note: The trick to getting finger-licking sticky but crisp golden pastry is either to have the syrup hot and pastry cool, or the syrup cool and pastry hot. Rose water can also be used to flavour the syrup, and finely chopped fresh green pistachios look great sprinkled over the top.

honey tart

This is a variation on the traditional treacle tarts I used to make when working in Yorkshire.

1 batch Sweet Short Honey Pastry (see below)
1 cup Clover or Farmhouse Honey
30 g butter
finely grated zest and juice of 1 lemon
80 g fresh whole breadcrumbs (about 8 slices)
1 teaspoon ground ginger
beaten egg to glaze

Preheat the oven to 190ºC. Roll out the pastry on a lightly floured surface and line a 20 cm loose-bottomed pie tin. Keep aside trimmings for decorating the tops. Place the pastry shell in the fridge to chill while making the filling.

Warm the honey, butter, zest and juice until the butter melts. Combine the breadcrumbs and ginger and stir through the honey mix. Fill the pastry base. Make strips from the reserved pastry and make a lattice top. Glaze with a little beaten egg. Bake for 25 minutes or until the filling is set.

SERVES 4–6.

2 cups standard flour
pinch salt
125 g butter
1 teaspoon baking powder
1 heaped tablespoon honey
1 egg yolk, lightly beaten
2 tablespoons dark rum
finely grated rind of 1 lemon
cold water with a squeeze of lemon juice to bind

Sweet short honey pastry

Place the flour, salt, butter, baking powder and honey in a food processor. Blend until a fine, even texture. Mix egg yolk, rum and rind with 1 tablespoon of the water. Add to the processor in pulses until just moist enough to draw together into a ball, adding more water if necessary. Knead lightly then roll out onto a floured board. Cut a 25 cm diameter circle. Place on a baking sheet and randomly prick with a fork. Chill for 10 minutes. Bake at 200ºC until golden.

Chef's note: For an unusual variation, add a little fresh rosemary, 1 teaspoon finely chopped, to the mix and decorate the top with a fresh sprig and a scattering of rosemary flowers. Remember that tarts do not have to be round: for a change try squares or rectangles.

fresh ginger cake

Honey and ginger are made to go together. This is a nice twist on a very traditional theme.

$\frac{1}{2}$ cup (100 g) butter, melted
$\frac{1}{2}$ cup thick natural yoghurt
$\frac{1}{2}$ cup Rewarewa Honey
$\frac{1}{2}$ cup sugar
2 eggs
grated rind of 1 lemon
4 teaspoons peeled and finely
    grated fresh ginger
2 cups standard flour
1 teaspoon baking soda
$\frac{1}{2}$ teaspoon salt

$\frac{1}{2}$ cup Rewarewa Honey
1 nip of Stone's Ginger Wine
    (or brandy) infused with
    3 slices of root ginger
juice of $\frac{1}{2}$ lemon

Preheat the oven to 180ºC. Grease a 20 cm square pan. In a medium bowl, combine the first seven ingredients. Stir until smooth. Sift in the flour, baking soda and salt. Stir to combine and spread in the prepared cake tin. Bake for approximately 30–35 minutes. Cool briefly, then turn out onto a rack.

I like to serve this with Honeyed Ginger (see page 17) and cream, a little heap of crystallised stem ginger with runny honey or maybe a little Warm Honey Syrup.

Warm honey syrup
Warm to blend, but do not boil. Pour over the warm cake.

honey shortbread

225 g butter, softened
50 g mild honey, warmed
    to soften
1 cup icing sugar
2 ½ cups plain flour
60 g cornflour
1 teaspoon vanilla extract

Preheat the oven to 150ºC. Cream the butter, honey and icing sugar. Then gradually add the flour, cornflour and the vanilla and mix until well combined. Roll out or cut in bars. Bake for 20–30 minutes until only just colouring on the edges. Cool on baking trays for 5 minutes before transferring to cooling racks. Serve dusted with icing sugar or decorated with chocolate.

Chef's notes: Other ingredients like chopped macadamias or finely chopped peel can be added for variety. For a crisper finish, sprinkle with castor sugar before baking. Alternatively, brush with a little more melted honey before baking if you want a glossy golden finish.

honey meringue topping

A flavoursome variation for the classic lemon meringue pie.

½ cup honey
⅛ teaspoon salt
1 egg white

Mix all the ingredients together and beat until stiff with an electric beater. This creates a softer meringue than sugar. Spread over the pie. Place in a slow oven (160ºC) until the desired degree of firmness and browning is achieved.

Chef's note: Honey Meringue Topping is great on rhubarb, or try something different like tamarillo and apple filling. Cook fruit with honey instead of sugar syrup, as the honey softens the acidity nicely. Honey meringue has a softer texture than sugar meringue and a richer colour and flavour. It will take longer to form soft peaks, and will brown at a lower temperature.

walnut bread

There are some ingredients that are so made for each other it is like a marriage. Walnuts and honey are like that and this combination is topped only by walnuts, honey and gooey French cheese. A single batch of this recipe works in my bread maker.

2 heaped teaspoons
  Sure Bake Yeast
1 ½ cups high-grade or strong
  flour
2 teaspoons sugar
2 tablespoons oil — walnut
  or canola
½ cup wholemeal flour
¾ teaspoon salt
2 tablespoons mild honey
  (see chef's notes)
¾ cup walnut pieces
¾ cup lukewarm water

If using the bread maker, place ingredients in the machine in this order. Otherwise place the lukewarm water, yeast, 2 tablespoons of the strong flour, sugar and oil in a bowl. Whisk to combine and leave in a warm place for a few minutes until the mixture becomes frothy. Meanwhile, mix the flours and salt and place in a large ceramic or glass bowl near somewhere warm.

When the yeast sponge is risen and frothy, warm the honey and whisk in then pour into a well made in the centre of the flour and mix gradually together to form a dough. Knead on a floured board until the dough is smooth and elastic and springs back when gently poked. Place in a lightly oiled bowl and cover with plastic wrap. Put aside in a warm place to rise until double in bulk. Depending on the temperature this may take 1 ½ –2 hours. Punch down the dough and knead until elastic, then add the walnuts. Shape and place in either oiled loaf tins or on a baking sheet for the second rise — approximately 30–45 minutes. Meanwhile, preheat the oven to 180ºC. Slash the tops of the dough and when ready to bake, lightly dust with extra flour and bake for 40–45 minutes until risen, nicely browned, firm and hollow-sounding when tapped.

Chef's notes: Take care when selecting your honey for yeast baking. Natural unheated treated honey, especially Manuka, will give poor results. The antibacterial properties of the honey will inhibit the yeast's growth, and result in a heavy loaf. Never place honey and yeast directly together. Choose a mild, even pasteurised, honey when working with yeast.

MAKES 1 LARGE LOAF OR 2 SMALLER LOAVES.

sesame seed brittle

Another Middle Eastern specialty. As children we looked with wonder at these exotic treats when they were first seen in New Zealand because sesame seeds were only ever used on dinner bread rolls. It was a long time before I could accept sweet sesame seeds. Once game enough to try, I was won over immediately.

1 ½ **cups sugar**
¼ **cup water**
½ **cup mild Farmhouse Honey**
2 cups sesame seeds

Line a Swiss roll tin with non-stick baking paper. Combine the sugar, water and honey in a heavy-bottomed medium pan. Stir over low heat, without boiling, until all the sugar is dissolved. Brush any sugar crystals from the side of the pan with a pastry brush dipped in water. When all the sugar is dissolved, increase the heat and bring to the boil. Boil uncovered without stirring until the mixture reaches soft ball stage (116°C) on a sugar thermometer (a teaspoon of mixture will form a soft ball when dropped into a cup of cold water). Remove from heat and allow bubbles to subside, then gently stir in the sesame seeds. Return the mixture to the boil, and simmer without stirring until the mixture reaches small crack stage (138°C) on the sugar thermometer (syrup forms a fine thread when dropped into cold water and can be snapped with fingers). Remove from the heat. Allow the bubbles to subside, then, taking special care because this mixture is very hot, pour into the prepared pan. Smooth and stand for 10 minutes, then mark in desired shapes. When completely cold, break into pieces. Store in an airtight container.

triple chocolate and honey truffles

Chocolate, honey and cream combined are a luxurious way to finish a meal. These also make a fabulous gift. If you prefer, dark chocolate may be substituted for the white in the filling.

**300 g white chocolate,
coarsely chopped**
150 ml cream
**50 g Tawari (or Pohutukawa)
Honey**
2 thinly peeled strips lemon rind
**200 g dark chocolate,
coarsely chopped**
**Dutch or baking cocoa
for dusting**

Process the white chocolate in a food processor until finely chopped. Combine the cream, honey and lemon rind in a small saucepan and bring to the boil, then discard the lemon rind. Pour the hot cream mixture over the chocolate in the food processor and blend until the chocolate has melted and the mixture is thick.

Transfer to a bowl and stand at room temperature for 30 minutes or until thick enough to shape. Either pipe into 7 mm x 25 mm sticks or gently roll into small balls. Place on baking paper and refrigerate for at least 1 hour until firm — overnight if possible.

Melt the dark chocolate in a bowl over hot water and stir until smooth. Working with a few at a time, dip the sticks or balls into the melted dark chocolate. Place the truffles back on the baking paper until set, then roll in cocoa powder. Store in an airtight container.

Chef's note: Try experimenting by adding some finely chopped peel, nuts or something like finely diced dried fruit or ginger to the filling.

honey and white chocolate panforte

This recipe is amazingly decadent and definitely not for those on diets. Sorry! However, it's still one of our all-time favourites and you can slice it very thinly for a flavour treat.

3 cups mixed glazed fruits (e.g. pineapple, papaya, mango, apricots, ginger, figs)
1 cup whole macadamia nuts
1 ¼ cups standard flour
1 ½ teaspoons ground cinnamon (or cardamom)
2 tablespoons water
½ cup mild honey
¾ cup sugar
100 g white chocolate
1 teaspoon vanilla
icing sugar to dust

Preheat the oven to 150ºC. Combine the fruit, nuts, flour and spice. Heat the water, honey and sugar slowly until the sugar has dissolved. Bring to the boil and simmer for 1 minute. Add the chocolate and vanilla, quickly stirring until smooth. Blend in all the dry ingredients. Press into a 20 cm square baking tin, which has been lined with baking paper or rice paper. Bake at 150ºC until set, with edges firm and centre still soft — approximately 45 minutes. Remove from the tin while still warm. Dust with icing sugar and cut into thin slices.

Store in an airtight container.

Chef's note: One edge of the panforte could be dipped in chocolate to finish.

Honey and White Chocolate Panforte,
Sesame Seed Brittle (see page 108)
and Triple Chocolate and Honey Truffles
(see page 109)

BeesOnline honeyed popcorn

2 tablespoons oil
60 g popping corn
2 tablespoons honey
¾ cup raw sugar
125 g butter

Heat the oil in a large pan, stir in the corn, cover and shake the pan constantly over heat until the popping stops. Remove the corn from the pan and cool. Place the corn in a lightly greased 20 cm x 30 cm lamington tin/Swiss roll tin or similar. Combine the honey, sugar and butter in a clean saucepan. Stir over low heat until the sugar is dissolved and the butter melted. Bring to the boil, then boil on medium heat for approximately 5 minutes or until the mixture is golden brown. Be careful — this mixture is very hot and quickly turns to caramel and can burn. Pour the honey mixture over the corn, and stir to coat well. Let it stand in a cool place until the honey is set, then break into serving-size pieces and store in an airtight container.

honeyed toffee walnuts

1 cup castor sugar
¼ cup honey
2 teaspoons water
2 cups (200 g) walnut halves
1 tablespoon sesame seeds

Cover an oven tray with baking paper. Combine the sugar, honey and water in a small pan and bring to the boil. Simmer uncovered until the syrup reaches 40ºC on a sugar thermometer or until golden brown. Stir in the walnuts and seeds. Spread the mixture over the prepared tray, separating the walnuts that are touching. When set, break apart any walnuts that stick together.

Keep stored in an airtight container at room temperature.

Best prepared on the day to be consumed.

clover honey fudge

This recipe is courtesy of Jo Seagar and comes from her book Jo Seagar's Nifty Tricks for Entertaining. *We suggest you try using BeesOnline Woodhill Clover Honey for this recipe. A sugar thermometer is essential for success.*

oil for spraying
1 ½ cups sugar
1 cup brown sugar
1 cup cream
2 tablespoons Clover Honey
50 g butter
1 teaspoon vanilla extract
½ cup chopped nuts (optional)

Line a 20 cm square cake tin with foil and spray with oil. Spray the sides of a medium to heavy saucepan with oil. Add both sugars, cream and honey to the saucepan and bring the mixture to the boil, stirring, over medium-high heat. At the soft ball stage (120ºC on a sugar thermometer), remove from the heat and add the butter and vanilla. Cool without stirring, until the mixture reaches 70ºC, then beat until it starts to thicken. (The electric handheld beater is great for this job.) Add the nuts and beat until the fudge starts to lose its gloss and becomes very thick. Quickly pour into the prepared tin. Score into squares while still warm. When cold, store in an airtight container.

honey and eucalyptus toffees

This recipe can be made a week ahead and the toffees kept in an airtight container at room temperature.

1 cup (250 g) castor sugar

½ cup water

1 tablespoon honey (try BeesOnline Farmhouse or Woodhill Clover)

2 teaspoons white vinegar or BeesOnline White Wine and Clover Honeygar

½ teaspoon eucalyptus oil

Place the sugar, water, honey and vinegar in a heavy-based pan. Stir over heat, without boiling, until the sugar is dissolved, brushing down the inside of the pan with a pastry brush dipped in hot water to remove sugar from the sides.

Bring to the boil, and simmer uncovered without stirring until the mixture reaches a temperature of 138°C on a sugar thermometer (or until a teaspoon of mixture dropped into a shallow bowl of cold water forms a fine thread which can be snapped with your fingers). Gently stir in the eucalyptus oil and strain into a heatproof jug.

Pour the syrup into 30 foil confectionery cases until half full. Stand until firm.

Remove foil cases. Wrap toffee in cellophane if desired.

MAKES APPROXIMATELY 30.

Viva honeycomb

Julie Biuso ran this classic school holiday favourite in the New Zealand Herald*'s Viva section several years ago.*

butter for greasing
3 tablespoons Clover Honey
1 tablespoon golden syrup
175 g castor sugar
3 tablespoons water
1 ¾ teaspoons baking soda

Children are always fascinated by the process of making honeycomb or hokey pokey, but they require constant supervision because the sugar gets very hot and can burn deeply if it gets on the skin.

Line a Swiss roll or roasting tin with greased baking paper. Put the honey, golden syrup, sugar and water in a saucepan. Set the pan over a low heat until the sugar dissolves. Do not stir — swirl the pan to dissolve the sugar evenly and do not let the mixture bubble before the sugar is dissolved. Bring to the boil, then lower the heat and let bubble and foam until it reaches 150ºC (around the hard crack stage) on a sugar thermometer. You can test this quickly by dropping a small amount into a cup of ice-cold water; it should snap, not be soft or bendy. Do not let the mixture go past 150ºC or it will burn. As soon as the syrup reaches 150ºC, remove it from the heat and, using a long-handled metal spoon, stir in the baking soda. It will immediately froth and foam (be sure to choose a saucepan deep enough for this to take place).

Pour the honeycomb into the prepared tin and leave it to cool. Break it into chunks and use immediately or transfer to an airtight container.

Chef's note: To ensure that the sugar thermometer does not shatter when you put it in the pan of dissolved sugar, warm it before use by standing it in a jug of hot water (dry it with a clean cloth before putting it into the pan of boiling syrup).

warm almond, honey and vanilla milk

I was first introduced to Warm Almond Milk by an Italian friend. In the south of Italy and in Sicily they have small rustic-looking almonds, with fabulous flavour. This makes an interesting warm winter's drink with a good protein base.

2 cups milk (low-fat can be used)
30 g ground almonds
1 tablespoon Wildflower Honey
1 teaspoon vanilla extract
4 pinches cinnamon

Combine the milk, ground almonds, honey and vanilla in a saucepan. Bring to the boil and remove from the heat. Blend in a food processor or blender until smooth and frothy. Pour into mugs and sprinkle with cinnamon.

SERVES 6.

fresh fruit daiquiris

½ cup of fresh fruit, peeled and roughly chopped (apricots, peaches, kiwifruit, nectarines or fresh berries)
1 tablespoon runny Clover Honey
2 cups crushed ice
1 tablespoon lemon or lime juice
¼ cup light rum

Blend the fresh fruit until smooth, then drizzle in the honey (if using kiwi fruit take care not to crush the seeds). Add the remaining ingredients and pulse until combined, but still crunchy. Serve immediately in a chilled glass.

SERVES 2.

Chef's note: Also great frozen for sorbet.

honey mead highball

Honey Mead Highballs have been on our beverage list since opening day. Judging by the number of regular imbibers I suspect it will be on the beverage list from now to ever after. Cheers to more lazy summer days!

½ **glass ice**
mint
⅔ **Havills chilled Honey Mead**
⅓ **ginger ale**
lemon slice

Place ice and mint in a blender and process until crushed and blended. Add mead and ginger ale and pour into a tall glass. Garnish with a slice of lemon.

SERVES 1.

honeyed spirulina cocktail

I use Life Stream Spirulina Powder, a biogenic wholefood concentrate of dehydrated, freshwater, blue-green microalgae. On a weight-for-weight basis, spirulina is a wholefood source of vitamins, minerals and amino acids, with extremely high digestibility. It's available from health-food shops.

1 cup orange juice (preferably freshly squeezed)
1 kiwi fruit
½**–1 banana**
1 teaspoon of your favourite honey
½**–1 teaspoon spirulina powder**

Put all in a blender and whiz until smooth and fluffy.

SERVES 1.

Chef's note: This recipe is suitable for vegetarians and vegans.

lemon concentrate

6 tablespoons Farmhouse Honey
1 cup strained lemon juice
slices of lemon

Dissolve the honey in the pure lemon juice, add slices of lemon and refrigerate.

In summer dilute with chilled still or carbonated water. In winter dilute with hot water.

Try this with oranges, tangelos or limes for a variation on the theme!

SERVES 1.

pear and pohutukawa honey smoothie

1 cup low-fat milk
2 tablespoons natural yoghurt
1 large ripe pear
1 egg
2 heaped teaspoons Pohutukawa
  Honey

Blend all until smooth and frothy. Serve with a little freshly grated nutmeg on the top.

SERVES 1.

rum toddy

Just the thing on a cold winter's evening, especially if you feel a cold coming on.

1 slice of lemon, studded with
  whole clove
juice of 1 lemon
1 heaped teaspoon Manuka
  Honey
1 nip dark rum (or whisky)

Combine all ingredients and top up with boiling water. Sip immediately.

SERVES 1.

Left: Honey Mead Highball
Middle: Warm Almond Honey
and Vanilla Milk
Right: Rum Toddy

index